The Power of the Dharma

The Power of the Dharma

✦

An Introduction to Hinduism and Vedic Culture

Stephen Knapp

iUniverse, Inc.
New York Lincoln Shanghai

The Power of the Dharma
An Introduction to Hinduism and Vedic Culture

iUniverse books may be ordered through booksellers or by contacting:

iUniverse
2021 Pine Lake Road, Suite 100
Lincoln, NE 68512
www.iuniverse.com
1-800-Authors (1-800-288-4677)

Cover: The Om, a name of God and the symbol of all creation; the beginning, middle and end, and the seed of all Vedic knowledge.

ISBN-13: 978-0-595-39352-7 (pbk)
ISBN-13: 978-0-595-83748-9 (ebk)
ISBN-10: 0-595-39352-7 (pbk)
ISBN-10: 0-595-83748-4 (ebk)

Printed in the United States of America

OTHER BOOKS BY THE AUTHOR

The Secret Teachings of the Vedas
The Universal Path to Enlightenment
The Vedic Prophecies: A New Look into the Future
How the Universe was Created and Our Purpose In It
Toward World Peace: Seeing the Unity Between Us All
Facing Death: Welcoming the Afterlife
Proof of Vedic Culture's Global Existence
The Key to Real Happiness
Destined for Infinity
Reincarnation and Karma: How They Really Affect Us
The Heart of Hinduism: The Eastern Path to Freedom, Empowerment and Illumination
Editor of Vedic Culture: The Difference It Can Make In Your Life

Find out more about Stephen Knapp, his articles, books and projects, and much additional information at his website:
www.Stephen-Knapp.com

Contents

Introduction

This is especially written for those who want an easy reference and introduction to the Vedic Hindu philosophy and tradition. This provides a concise overview and quick guide of the major principles found within Vedic culture. It answers the most common questions people have about Vedic customs and its Dharmic teachings. It also offers a good grasp of the essential values and ideology of the Vedic path while keeping it simple to understand.

This book also serves as an introduction to deeper reading that a person may like to do in considering the more elaborate explanations of the Vedic/Hindu philosophy. And as an introduction or a companion to other books by Stephen Knapp, such as *The Secret Teachings of the Vedas: The Eastern Answers to the Mysteries of Life*, which is a good in-depth analysis and exposition of the Vedic spirituality and philosophy, and *The Heart of Hinduism: The Eastern Path to Freedom, Empowerment and Illumination*, which is a complete course in itself for learning exactly what Hinduism and Vedic culture teaches. Descriptions of these and other books are provided in the back of this volume. So if this book piques your interest and you are inquisitive to learn more about the deeper aspects of Vedic spirituality, those are the books that can take you much farther in this spiritual knowledge and awareness.

1

What Is Vedic Culture/Hinduism

Vedic culture, more popularly known as Hinduism today, has spread everywhere and is followed by over one billion people around the world. Every seventh person in the world is a follower of the Vedic tradition, which equals 13.7% of the population. Even now an increasing number of people, especially in the West, are following its principles and avenues of spiritual Self-discovery, such as yoga and its tenets. Vedic culture continues to be broad-minded and provide the oldest of wisdom and a highly developed philosophy. Those who follow the Vedic spiritual path known as Sanatana-dharma or the Dharma are often called Hindus, but also can be known as Dharmists or Dharmis.

Vedic culture is the indigenous culture of India. It is not merely a code of religion but a way of life with something for anyone, regardless of what level of consciousness or inquiry into spiritual truths that a person may have. Vedic Dharma encourages and provides the means for a person to understand and recognize God in all of creation. It is universal and applicable for everyone and is based on the eternal principles of spiritual knowledge. This is why it is called Sanatana-dharma, which means the eternal nature of the soul that transcends time and location. Vedic Dharma is based on the Vedic texts, which are the most ancient of all literature in the world. It is supplied for the benefit of all humanity, with the intention that is explained in the *Kathopanishad* (2.6.19): "May all be happy, may all be free from disease, may all realize what is good, and may none be subject to misery."

So what does it mean to follow this Vedic path? It generally means to learn the ways of a spiritually progressed person. This includes understanding one's spiritual identity, knowing that he or she is not the temporary body but is spirit soul, that there is karma or reactions for one's activities, and rebirth in another life after death in which one reaps the reward or punishment for his or her own good or evil thoughts, words and deeds. By having a solid understanding of such spiritual knowledge, there is automatically a respect for all others regardless of their

1

race, sex, position, or species. This can bring a moral and peaceful behavior in everybody toward everyone. By having respect for everyone's spiritual identity, this also brings an innate happiness in us all. We can understand that we are only visiting this planet for a short time, and that we are all in this together. In other words, my contribution to your well-being, especially spiritual well-being, will be an automatic contribution to my own existence. In this way, society at large is in a state of constant improvement. Thus, together we all work toward attaining a clean mind and a pure heart. That is the goal of the Vedic way of life and all those who seriously follow it.

Many people find it difficult or impossible to define Vedic culture in a concise or adequate manner. It differs quite a bit from the conventional and western monotheistic religions with which many people are familiar. Hinduism is monotheistic in the sense that it accepts one Absolute Truth or Supreme Being, but in other ways it is pluralistic. In other words, it does not claim that there is only one prophet or savior, or only one holy book, one way to realize God, one way to be "saved", or only one life in which to do that. Instead, it includes all aspects of God; it does not subscribe to any one philosophy or dogma; it includes various schools of thought and ways of understanding spiritual Truth; it includes a variety of religious rites or sacraments; it can include any scripture that can help a person understand more about God and spiritual Truth; and it does not say that you have only one life in which to become spiritually perfect or you will go to eternal damnation. Thus, Vedic philosophy is more of a way of living and an outlook on life than a religion.

Because of this, Hinduism and the path of Vedic culture includes a variety of customs, ideas and philosophies. It accommodates a wide range of approaches for allowing people to advance and understand our spiritual identity and transcendental Truth. It allows everyone to question the scriptures to increase one's understanding, and recognizes no single person or prophet as having an exclusive claim over the Absolute Truth. Everyone can follow a system of realization to approach God since this is everyone's right and destiny, and use the approach that is most suitable for them in this life. The Vedic process recognizes that everyone is evolving through different levels of consciousness and thus needs different methods of understanding the Absolute Truth. This flexibility is one of the reasons why Vedic culture has continued over so many thousands of years.

This is also why many variations of philosophical thought or schools of religion can be viewed as branches or tributaries of the same great river of Sanatana-dharma, which is the universal spiritual knowledge and practice that are the essential teachings of the Vedic literature. Such spiritual knowledge can be recognized in many forms of religion or their scripture. Because of this, it also means that no one is excluded or excommunicated from the Hindu or Vedic path. There are no heretics, but there is room for everyone and respect for all who are practicing its basic principles of spiritual pursuit and understanding. This is also one reason why Hindus generally get along with other religions, though there have been many who have taken unfair advantage of their amiable nature.

So Vedic culture is not an organized religion like Christianity or Islam. It has no single founder. It has no Pope. It has no hierarchy, though people do recognize particular spiritual authorities or gurus. It also has numerous scriptures. And in some of these Vedic texts you are actually studying the history and culture of India, just as through the 39 books of the Old Testament of the Bible you are studying the culture and history of the Jews.

As we examine the broader perspective of religion and spiritual paths throughout the world, such as the shamanic and tribal views, we find much that is connected with the Vedic perspective. Thus, Vedic culture contains the deep roots of spirituality which existed before the entrance of the limiting dogmas that we presently find dominating much of the world. And these roots will once again emerge as mankind searches for deeper levels of spiritual understanding, beyond the dogmas in religions that confine or restrict one's inquiry into the Infinite by instilling the exclusivist idea that anything beyond what it offers is evil or bad. Truth and the sincere search for it can never be anything but a positive development.

Hinduism and Judaism are the sources of all modern religions in the world. Buddhism, Sikhism and to some extent Jainism and Zoroastrianism were outgrowths from Hinduism. Of course, Jainism existed during the period of the *Rig Veda*. Statues of Rishabha, the first Thirthankara and founder of Jainism, were found in the Mohenjadaro and Harappa excavations. Judaism, Islam and Christianity have Abraham as the common father figure. All three have many common prophets.

C.S. Lewis, the great author and theologist accurately explained, "Finally it will come to two religions. Hinduism and Christianity. The first [Hinduism] will grow absorbing ideas and concepts from everywhere and later [Christianity] will keep away from everything that is foreign to it." This is one reason why Hinduism has continued for so many years and cannot be destroyed, even if we burn every Vedic scripture and kill every Hindu theologian on earth. Hinduism or Vedic culture is a very dynamic, living, breathing reality. The strength of Hinduism lies in its most amazing ability to adapt to different circumstances and different ages while maintaining its strong continuity with the past and its timeless spiritual knowledge and principles.

THE SIMPLE DEFINITION OF HINDUISM

More than anything else, Hinduism or the Vedic path is the simple search for Truth without the insistence or demand that Truth be described in only one particular belief or a single way. This is why Sanatana-dharma is also called Satya-dharma, meaning the search for or religion of Truth. One can search for Truth in a number of different ways and still be considered a Hindu or a follower of Sanatana-dharma. Very few religions will or can say that. It is a universal teaching that anyone can utilize as a means of attaining spiritual knowledge and personal perception. Its highest ideal is the liberation from material existence of the individual, and all those who are willing to understand the means to attain it through spiritual consciousness.

WHAT HINDUISM IS NOT

Hinduism is not organized in the way we see most religions in the world. It does not have a particular founder, savior, book, leader or holy place. It has no specific day of the week to observe, or call to prayer, or certain ritual that everyone must observe. It is decentralized and localized in a way in which it allows anyone to observe the basic principles that are best for him or her. Often, rather than worshiping in a temple, Hindus make temples in their own homes. Thus, Hinduism is an open path that appeals to those who prefer the great diversity of its teachings and does not require an exclusive regimen. In other words, Hinduism is a path that respects the individual and one's own approach and development over and above that of a centralized committee or sacred capital wherein the dictates of the religion are pronounced.

However, the teachings of the Vedic path are most organized for step-by-step progress. Its teachings and philosophy are very structured and encompass all aspects of human life. However, one is free to approach them from any angle or to supplement them in one's life as best as he or she sees fit. This is also why some of the most noted of Western thinkers, such as Thoreau, Emerson, Goethe, Schopenhauer, and others have viewed Vedanta as one of the greatest of spiritual philosophies.

THE VERSATILITY OF HINDUISM

Vedic Dharma is not a single religion as most people think. You will probably find no greater variety of religions or sects within any religion as in Hinduism. You will find the Vaishnavas (worshippers of Vishnu and Krishna), Shaivites (worshippers of Shiva) Shaktas (worshippers of the Goddess), Ganapatas (worshippers of Ganesh), or the Brahmavadis (those who consider the impersonal Brahman as the ultimate), and others. There are also a variety of rituals, prayers and outlooks, such as monotheism, polytheism, agnosticism, atheism, monism, and so on. For this reason you also find a wider variety of religions in India than almost anywhere else. In fact, you will find more Islamic sects within India than in any Islamic country in the world, even those factions that are banned in other Islamic countries. The point is that Sanatana-dharma is a collection of approaches to different aspects of the Absolute Truth, depending on what aspect a person feels he or she needs the most. However, each Vedic path is connected to the other and they all share the basic principles of the Vedic tradition.

Another difference in the Vedic path or Sanatana-dharma is that it does not force non-Hindus to give up their own ways or culture, but it encourages that we assist each other in a broader search for spiritual Truth. This search can be done in many ways, which the Vedic tradition includes and describes. Vedic Dharma is not an intolerant process. It accepts all great teachers and teachings for their value in assisting everyone to better understand the Absolute Truth, and to help us reach our own level of Self-realization. We can all share our spiritual knowledge to realize God. The Dharma does not demand social conformity but aims to provide the means and knowledge that is the way of realizing the Self within.

Vedic Dharma does not try to fix the path of understanding the Absolute to only one way or to a single form. Different ways work better for different people, depending on their level of consciousness, past experience and the lessons they may need to learn in this lifetime.

Furthermore, Hindus are not restricted from studying other religions or philosophies, or in respecting any aspect of Truth wherever they may recognize it. You will not find people labeled heretics, kafirs, pagans, apostates, and so on in Hinduism. There are no blanket restrictions handed down by some Pope, or any process of excommunication, or the idea that one will go to hell for improperly following the path. Also, Hindus do not try to force others to convert from another religion, nor have they ever invaded another country for religious purposes.

Hindus only encourage others to look more deeply into understanding the universal spiritual Truth of which everyone is a part. For this, they do not consider holding diverse views as something negative, but only ways of viewing different aspects of the Divine. Everyone may have and share their own insights and, thus, gain clarity into the nature of the Absolute Truth. Using intelligence and honest thinking is what is respected rather than merely repeating the sayings or the impositions of others.

WHO FOUNDED VEDIC CULTURE

No one individual founded Vedic culture, nor is there any single prophet, holy book or way of worship. The Vedic Dharma has a library of texts to help establish the nature of the Absolute Truth. Hindus recognize the good and spiritual essence in all religions, so it is easy for them to display respect and tolerance for other spiritual paths.

Through the Puranic stories of the universal creation, we learn that the Vedic knowledge was *shabda-brahma*, or a spiritual vibration that existed both within and beyond the fabric of the universe. It was first given by Lord Vishnu to the secondary creator and first living being known as Brahma. It was Brahma who then disseminated it to other great sages and masters, the rishis. It is through the continued research and output of these learned rishis that humanity has learned the various levels of spiritual Truth, as they have been handed down through the generations.

VEDIC CULTURE STARTED BEFORE THE BEGINNING OF TIME

To explain further from the previous point, nobody knows when Vedic culture started. It goes back to before the beginning of history. If you go by the Vedic legends and histories, Vedic culture is trillions of years old. It is said to have originally been a vibration, an eternal and pure spiritual vibration known as *shabda-brahma*. This existed eternally before the material creation ever manifested. This spiritual vibration was first articulated to humanity by God. It is said that through this spiritual vibration one can understand the Supreme. This vibration descended from the spiritual domain and pervades the fabric of the material strata. Thus, those great sages who have become spiritually realized can receive and perceive this spiritual vibration. Then they work to reveal that to others through their writings and descriptions of the path by which one can be spiritually enlightened themselves. This was the start of the Vedic philosophy and its system of knowledge.

According to Vedic scriptures, this revelation of the spiritual vibration started as *shruti*—that which is heard. It was passed on as a vocal tradition. The great seers of ancient times called rishis who had perfected themselves have heard in their hearts the eternal truths and taught those truths to disciples by telepathy and talks, and later through writings in books which became known as the *Vedas* and *Upanishads*. These are known as the *shruti* literature. The remaining part of the Vedic literature is called *smriti*, or that which is remembered. These are all supplements and elaborations of the Vedic truths. All these Vedic scriptures were considered as revealed truths from God.

Even if you accept the conclusions of Max Mueller, the German philosopher, Vedic culture and its knowledge is at least 8000 to 9000 years old. However, studying the relics of Mohenjadaro and Harappa excavations, the Indus Valley civilization shows the seeds from which arose many other cultures and concepts. The Indus Valley was home to the largest of the four ancient urban civilizations of Egypt, Mesopotamia, India and China. Harappa and Mohenjodaro were cities in the Indus Valley civilization that flourished around 2,500 B.C. in the western part of South Asia. The roots of Vedic culture can be traced to this area of civilization and even earlier. It has spread throughout the world and has been used by many other cultures, many of which were once a part of, or related to, Vedic Dharma. That is why you can see the influence of Vedic culture in the relics of all other civilizations like the Egyptian, Celtic, Mayan, Greek, Roman, etc. I have analyzed this more completely in another book called "Proof of Vedic Culture's Global Existence".

2

Quotes by Noteworthy People On the Glories of Vedic Culture

Vedic culture and its spiritual lifestyle, the Dharma, have been appreciated for many years by many scholars and people in general. There are many quotes expressing such appreciation that could be supplied, but we will review a few of these to show the typical sentiment that many such people have had toward India and what it has given the world.

For example, in *Greater India* by Arun Bhattacharjee (inside cover) he declared, "So now we turn to India. This spiritual gift, that makes a man human, is still alive in Indian souls. Go on giving the world Indian examples of it. Nothing else can do so much to help mankind to save itself from destruction."

The great British historian Dr. Arnold Joseph Toynbee (1889-1975) also agreed with this sentiment. He was a great writer and published his massive research in 12 volumes between 1934 and 1961, called *A Study of History*. He was also the author of several books, including *Christianity: Among the Religions of the World* and *One World and India*. In commenting on India and the Vedic Hindu religion, he said: "It is already becoming clear that a chapter which had a Western beginning will have to have an Indian ending if it is not to end in self-destruction of the human race. At this supremely dangerous moment in human history, the only way of salvation is the ancient Hindu way. Here we have the attitude and spirit that can make it possible for the human race to grow together into a single family."

Toynbee also recognized how India was the source of the major religious philosophies that had spread throughout the Mediterranean region. He said, "India is not only the heir of her own religious traditions; she is also the residuary legatee of the Ancient Mediterranean World's religious traditions...Religion cuts far deeper, and, at the religious level, India has not been a recipient; she has been a giver. About half the total number of the living higher religions are of Indian origin." [1]

Toynbee also recognized the tolerance of Hinduism, who on many occasions contrasted the exclusivity of the Jewish tradition, based on the Jewish belief that the Jews are the chosen people. He claimed that this plague of exclusiveness was inherited by both the Christians and Muslims: hence their lamentable record. [2]

Another admirer of Vedic culture was Henry Thoreau. He had commented on it in several sources, such as this: "In the morning I bathe my intellect in the stupendous and cosmogonal philosophy of the Bhagavat Geeta, since whose composition years of the gods have elapsed, and in comparison with which our modern world and its literature seem puny and trivial; and I doubt if that philosophy is not to be referred to a previous state of existence, so remote is its sublimity from our conceptions. I lay down the book and go to my well for water, and lo! there I meet the servant of the Brahmin, priest of Brahma, and Vishnu and Indra, who still sits in his temple on the Ganges reading the Vedas, or dwells at the root of a tree with his crust and water-jug. I meet his servant come to draw water for his master, and our buckets as it were grate together in the same well. The pure Walden water is mingled with the sacred water of the Ganges."

At Walden he put the Bhagavad Gita to the test, while proving to his generation that "money is not required to buy one necessary for the soul." [3] "How much more admirable the Bhagavad Geeta than all the ruins of the East." [4]

Schopenhauer was another who had been greatly impressed by the Vedic tradition of India. He wrote that, "From every sentence (of the Upanishads) deep, original and sublime thoughts arise, and the whole is pervaded by a high and holy and earnest spirit…In the whole world there is no study so beneficial and so elevating as that of the Upanishads. They are destined sooner or later to become the faith of the people."

Schopenhauer, who was in the habit, before going to bed, of performing his devotions from the pages of the *Upanishads*, regarded them in this way: "It has been the solace of my life—it will be the solace of my death." [5]

In the preface of his book *The World as a Will and Representation*, Schopenhauer wrote: "According to me, the influence of Sanskrit literature on our time will not be lesser than what was in the 16th century Greece's influence on Renaissance. One day, India's wisdom will flow again on Europe and will totally transform our knowledge and thought."

We certainly cannot forget Emerson and his thoughts on the Vedic texts. He was most impressed by the *Bhagavad-gita*, the *Upanishads* and other scriptures of India. Of the *Bhagavad-gita* he said: "I owed a magnificent day to the Bhagavad-

Geeta. It was as if an empire spoke to us, nothing small or unworthy, but large, serene, consistent, the voice of an old intelligence which in another age and climate had pondered and thus disposed of the same questions which exercise us." [6]

In his Journal, Emerson paid homage to Vedic thought in this way: "It is sublime as night and a breathless ocean. It contains every religious sentiment, all the grand ethics which visit in turn each noble poetic mind…It is of no use to put away the book; if I trust myself in the woods or in a boat upon the pond. Nature makes a Brahmin of me presently: eternal compensation, unfathomable power, unbroken silence…This is her creed. Peace, she saith to me, and purity and absolute abandonment—these panaceas expiate all sin and bring you to the beatitude of the Eight Gods." [7]

The Theosophist Annie Besant, who had been a friend of Swami Vivekananda, had also acquired a great appreciation for Hinduism and the tradition of India. She had boldly said: "After a study of some forty years and more of the great religions of the world, I find none so perfect, none so scientific, none so philosophical and none so spiritual than the great religion known by the name of Hinduism. Make no mistake, without Hinduism, India has no future. Hinduism is the soil in to which India's roots are stuck and torn out of that she will inevitably wither as a tree torn out from its place. And if Hindus do not maintain Hinduism who shall save it? If India's own children do not cling to her faith who shall guard it. India alone can save India and India and Hinduism are one." [8]

Annie Besant also expressed that, "Among the priceless teachings that may be found in the great Indian epic Mahabharata, there is none so rare and priceless as the Gita…This is the India of which I speak—the India which, as I said, is to me the Holy Land. For those who, though born for this life in a Western land and clad in a Western body, can yet look back to earlier incarnations in which they drank the milk of spiritual wisdom from the breast of their true mother—they must feel ever the magic of her immemorial past, must dwell ever under the spell of her deathless fascination; for they are bound to India by all the sacred memories of their past; and with her, too, are bound up all the radiant hopes of their future, a future which they know they will share with her who is their true mother in the soul-life." [9]

Mrs. Besant remarked during her lecture at the Grand Theatre in Calcutta on Jan 15th, 1906: "India is the mother of religion. In her are combined science and religion in perfect harmony, and that is the Hindu religion, and it is India that shall be again the spiritual mother of the world." [10]

The impressive nature of the Vedic tradition did not go unnoticed by early French thinkers. Victor Cousin (1792-1867) eminent French philosopher, whose knowledge of the history of European philosophy was unrivalled, believes that: "When we read with attention the poetical and philosophical monuments of the East—above all, those of India, which are beginning to spread in Europe—we discover there many a truth, and truths so profound, and which make such a contrast with the meanness of the results at which European genius has sometimes stopped, that we are constrained to bend the knee before the philosophy of the East, and to see in this cradle of the human race the native land of the highest philosophy." [11]

Another American historian, Will Durant (1885-1981) thought that the West should learn from India its tolerance and gentleness and love for all living things. He said: "It is true that even across the Himalayan barrier India has sent to us such questionable gifts as grammar and logic, philosophy and fables, hypnotism and chess, and above all our numerals and our decimal system. But these are not the essence of her spirit; they are trifles compared to what we may learn from her in the future."

"Perhaps in return for conquest, arrogance and spoliation, India will teach us the tolerance and gentleness of the mature mind, the quiet content of the unacquisitive soul, the calm of the understanding spirit, and a unifying, pacifying love for all living things." [12]

Will Durant also said: "India was the motherland of our race, and Sanskrit the mother of Europe's languages: she was the mother of our philosophy; mother, through the Arabs, of much of our mathematics; mother, through the Buddha, of the ideals embodied in Christianity; mother, through the village community, of self-government and democracy. Mother India is in many ways the mother of us all. Nothing should more deeply shame the modern student than the recency and inadequacy of his acquaintance with India....This is the India that patient scholarship is now opening up like a new intellectual continent to that Western mind which only yesterday thought civilization an exclusive Western thing."

Aldous Huxley (1894-1963) is another distinguished person known for having been most impressed with the wisdom of the East. The English novelist and essayist, born into a family that included some of the most distinguished members of the English ruling class, had said that the *Bhagavad-gita* is for the whole world. Author of several books including *Brave New World* and *The Doors of Perception and Heaven and Hell* and *The Perennial Philosophy*, he observed: "The Bhagavad-Gita is the most systematic statement of spiritual evolution of endowing value to mankind. The Gita is one of the clearest and most comprehensive summaries of the spiritual thoughts ever to have been made." [13]

Furthermore, Huxley wrote in his book, *The Perennial Philosophy* that "The religions whose theology is least preoccupied with events in time and most concerned with eternity, have been consistently less violent and more humane in political practice. Unlike early Judaism, Christianity and Mohammedanism (all obsessed with time) Hinduism and Buddhism have never been persecuting faiths, have preached almost no holy wars and have refrained from that proselytizing religious imperialism which has gone hand in hand with political and economic oppression of colored people." [14]

It is agreed by any scholar of history or religion that the earliest spiritual writings that can be found are the Vedic *samhitas*, such as the *Rig-veda*. In *History of Ancient Sanskrit Literature* (page 557), Max Müeller observed, "In the *Rig-veda* we shall have before us more real antiquity than in all the inscriptions of Egypt or Ninevah…the *Veda* is the oldest book in existence…"

In the same book (page 63) Max Müeller also noted, "The *Veda* has a two-fold interest: It belongs to the history of the world and to the history of India. In the history of the world the *Veda* fills a gap which no literary work in any other language could fill. It carries us back to times of which we have no records anywhere."

When turning to Friedrich Maximilian Müeller (1823-1900) German philologist and Orientalist, it is known that he had his own deceitful agenda for dealing with the Sanskrit literature of India. However, he could not ignore the impressive thoughts and philosophy that they held. He repeatedly drew the attention of the uniqueness of the Vedic literature among his educated friends. Müeller is best known for his series *Sacred Books of the East*, in which he wrote: "If I were asked under what sky the human mind has most fully developed some of its choicest gifts, has most deeply pondered over the greatest problems of life, and has found solutions of some of them which well deserve the attention even of those who have studied Plato and Kant, I should point to India. And if I were to ask myself from what literature we who have been nurtured almost exclusively on the thoughts of Greeks and Romans, and of the Semitic race, the Jewish, may draw the corrective which is most wanted in order to make our inner life more perfect, more comprehensive, more universal, in fact more truly human a life…again I should point to India." [15]

In other places Müeller had written: "I maintain that for everybody who cares for himself, for his ancestors, for his history, for his intellectual development, a study of Vedic literature is indispensable."

"The *Upanishads* are the…sources of…the Vedanta philosophy, a system in which human speculation seems to me to have reached its very acme…I spend my happiest hours in reading Vedantic books. They are to me like the light of the morning, like the pure air of the mountains—so simple, so true, if once understood."

"Historical records (of the Hindus) extend in some respects so far beyond all records and have been preserved to us in such perfect and legible documents, that we can learn from them lessons which we can learn nowhere else and supply missing links." [16]

Max Müeller is also quoted as having said that: "The Vedic literature opens to us a chamber in the education of human race to which we can find no parallel anywhere else. Whoever cares for the historical growth of our language and thought, whoever cares for the first intelligent development of religion and mythology, whoever cares for the first foundation of Science, Astronomy, Metronomy, Grammar and Etymology, whoever cares for the first intimation of the first philosophical thoughts, for the first attempt at regulating family life, village life and state life as founded on religion, ceremonials, traditions and contact must in future pay full attention to the study of Vedic literature." [17]

Modern scientists also have not let the Vedic tradition go unnoticed. The famous astronomer Carl Sagan says: "The most elegant and sublime of these is a representation of the creation of the universe at the beginning of each cosmic cycle, a motif known as the cosmic dance of Lord Shiva. The god, called in this manifestation Nataraja, the Dance King. In the upper right hand is a drum whose sound is the sound of creation. In the upper left hand is a tongue of flame, a reminder that the universe, now newly created, with billions of years from now will be utterly destroyed."

"These profound and lovely images are, I like to imagine, a kind of premonition of modern astronomical ideas." Sagan continues, "A millennium before Europeans were willing to divest themselves of the Biblical idea that the world was a few thousand years old, the Mayans were thinking of millions and the Hindus billions." [18]

In the episode entitled "The Edge of Forever" in the "Cosmos" television series, Carl Sagan visits India, and by way of introducing some of the bizarre ideas of modern physics, he acknowledges that of all the world's philosophies and religions, those originating in India are remarkably consistent with contemporary scenarios of space, time and existence.

In his book *Broca's Brain: Reflections on the Romance of Science*, he remarks:

"Immanuel Velikovsky (the author of *Earth in Upheaval*) in his book *Worlds in Collision*, notes that the idea of four ancient ages terminated by catastrophe is common to Indian as well as to Western sacred writing. However, in the *Bhaga-*

vad Gita and in the *Vedas*, widely divergent numbers of such ages, including an infinity of them, are given; but, more interesting, the duration of the ages between major catastrophes is specified as billions of years."

"The idea that scientists or theologians, with our present still puny understanding of this vast and awesome cosmos, can comprehend the origins of the universe is only a little less silly than the idea that Mesopotamian astronomers of 3,000 years ago–from whom the ancient Hebrews borrowed, during the Babylonian captivity, the cosmological accounts in the first chapter of Genesis–could have understood the origins of the universe. We simply do not know."

Thus, with only a few references to the views of some of the world's great thinkers, we can see the high regard that has been given toward India and its Vedic culture throughout the ages. In this way, there is no less reason to consider what it still and has always offered to the world. So let us take a closer look at the basis of the Vedic teachings.

CHAPTER NOTES

1. *One World and India*—By Arnold Toynbee, Indian Council for Cultural Relations, New Delhi. 1960 p 42-59

2. *Concordant Discord*—By R. C. Zaehner p 22-23

3. *The Writings of Henry D. Thoreau*—*Walden 1989*, Princeton Univ. Press. p 298

4. Ibid., p 57

5. *The Discovery of India*—By Jawaharlal Nehru, Oxford University Press. 1995. pg 92; and *The Upanishads, Translated for the Modern Reader*, By Eknath Easwaran Nilgiri Press,1987 p. 300; and *Outlines of Hinduism*—By T. M. P. Mahadevan—p.30).

6. *Philosophy of Hinduism*—*An Introduction*—By T. C. Galav, Universal Science-Religion, p 65; and *Hinduism*—By Linda Johnsen, p 42; and *Hindu Scriptures and American Transcendentalists*—By Umesh Patri, p 22-23).

7. *India's Priceless Heritage*—By Nani A. Palkhivala, 1980, p 9-24.

8. (Written in the cover notes from the book, *Hindus, Life-Line of India*, by G. M. Jagtiani.)

9. (from: *India: Essays and Lectures* Vol. IV—By Annie Besant, London, The Theosophical Publishing Co., p.11,1895)

10. *Hindu Superiority*—By Har Bilas Sarda

11. *Is India Civilized: Essays on Indian Culture*—By Sir John Woodroffe, p.132

12. *Philosophy of Hinduism—An Introduction*—By T. C. Galav, Universal Science-Religion, p 20

13. Ibid., p.65

14. *The Perennial Philosophy*—By Aldous Huxley, p.194-204

15. *The World's Religions*—By Huston Smith, Harper San Francisco, 1991, p.12

16. *India—What It Can Teach Us*—By Max Müeller, p.21

17. *Hinduism: The Eternal Religion*—By M. D. Chaturvedi, p.12-13

18. *Cosmos*—By Carl Sagan, p. 213-214

3

The Essential Principles
Of the Vedic Path

The best way to begin understanding the various aspects of Vedic culture is to look over the basic tenets. These are not so difficult to understand when we view them as such. These are like the codes that pave the way for a broader perspective of what Vedic culture has to offer. And one can easily see the universal nature of the Vedic teachings as well. Most people find them easily acceptable. Yet they also represent deep spiritual truths, which is why more elaborate explanations of these principles or codes of life will follow in the next chapter.

1. The Vedic Tradition or Hinduism is more than a religion, but a way of life, a complete philosophy for the foundation and direction for one's existence.

2. It is based on Universal Spiritual Truths that can be applied to anyone at anytime.

3. It is called Sanatana-dharma, the eternal nature of the soul.

4. It recognizes that there is one Supreme Being with no beginning or end, the all in all, the unlimited Absolute Truth, who can expand into many forms.

5. All life is supported by and is part of the one great Truth, known as Brahman, eternal, fully conscious and joyful. This Supreme, eternal consciousness is transcendental and simultaneously manifests its true nature as both a personal deity and impersonal energy, as well as both male and female forms.

6. The Divine Intelligence which supports all existence can and has appeared throughout history in the form of personal appearances (*avataras*) within the realm of matter, and even in the sound vibration of scriptures (the Vedic literature).

7. That Supreme Being is found in the spiritual dimension but also lives in the heart of all living beings.

8. The Vedic tradition recognizes that the individual soul is eternal, beyond the limitations of the body, and that one soul is no different than another.

9. The soul incarnates through different forms (called *samsara* or reincarnation) until it reaches liberation (*moksha*) from the repetition of birth and death, and attains its natural position in the spiritual domain.

10. The ultimate purpose of human life is to shed all attachments to matter and attain *moksha* (liberation from material existence) and return to the transcendental realm which is not only our true nature but also our real home.

11. All living entities, both human and otherwise, are the same in their essential and divine spiritual being. All of them are parts of the eternal truth, and have appeared in this world to express their nature and also to gather experience in the realms of matter.

12. For this reason, Vedic followers accept the premise of *Vasudhaiva Kutumbakam,* that all living beings in the universe comprise one family, and that as such all beings are spiritually equal and should be respected as members within that family of the Supreme.

13. Every person's capacity to spiritually progress depends upon their personal qualities, choices and abilities, and is not limited by the circumstances of one's color, caste, class or any other circumstance of birth or temporary material limitation or designations.

14. The Vedic path is based on regaining our natural spiritual identity. To pursue this goal, all human beings have the eternal right to choose their personal form of spiritual practice, as well as the right to reject any form of religious activity, and that coercion, forced conversion or commercial inducement should never be used or tolerated to present, propagate or enforce one's spiritual beliefs on others.

15. The Vedic path offers personal freedom for one to make his or her own choice of how he or she wants to pursue their spiritual approach, and what level of the Absolute Truth he or she wishes to understand. This is spiritual democracy and freedom from tyranny.

16. Recognizing the value and sanctity of all forms of life, as well as the Eternal Divine Being that is their true Self, the Vedic principle is that we should therefore strive in every possible way to peacefully co-exist with all other species of living entities.

17. The soul undergoes it's own karma, the law of cause and effect, by which each person creates his own destiny based on his thought, words and deeds. The soul undergoes this karma in the rounds of reincarnation. All beings that exist are subject to and will ultimately be held accountable to these Laws of Nature, which are of Divine Origin.

18. Material nature was designed and created, and is maintained and finally destroyed, by the purposeful actions of an all-pervading Divine Intelligence. The realms of matter are endlessly cyclic in nature. They are created, maintained for some time, annihilated and then begun again.

19. The processes and functions of material Nature are assisted by Divine Helpers (*devas*) who, though invisible to us, are real and with whom we live in a reciprocal relationship of mutual responsibility.

20. The Vedic path has a complete library of ancient texts known as the Vedic literature that explain these truths and the reasons for the tradition.

21. This Vedic literature is considered to be non-ordinary books that are the basis of the Vedic system. Some of these have been given or spoken by God, and others were composed by sages in their deepest super conscious state in which they were able to give revelations of Universal Truths while in meditation on the Supreme.

22. The Vedic literature provides the spiritual knowledge and instructions for assisting all living beings in their material and spiritual development and understanding.

23. This Vedic literature, including, among other texts, the *Rig, Sama, Yajur* and *Atharva Vedas*, the *Upa-Vedas, Vedangas, Shadarshanas, Upanishads*, the *Vedanta-Sutras, Yoga Sutras, Agamas*, the *Ramayana*, the *Mahabharata* and *Bhagavad-gita*, and all Puranic literature and the practices congruent with them, contain the basis of the Hindu/Sanatana-dharma spiritual culture.

24. The Vedic path consists of ten general rules of moral conduct. There are five for inner purity, called the *yamas*—*satya* or truthfulness, *ahimsa* or non-injury to others and treating all beings with respect, *asteya* or no cheating or stealing, *brahmacharya* or celibacy, and *aparighara* or no selfish accumulation of resources for one's own purpose. The five rules of conduct for external purification are the *niyamas*—*shaucha* or cleanliness and purity of mind and body, *tapas* or austerity and perseverance, *swadhyaya* or study of the *Vedas*, and *santosh* or contentment, as well as *ishvara-pranidhana*, acceptance of the Supreme.

25. There are also ten qualities that are the basis of *dharmic* (righteous) life. These are *dhriti* (firmness or fortitude), *kshama* (forgiveness), *dama* (self-control), *asteya* (refraining from stealing or dishonesty), *shauch* (purity), *indriya nigraha* (control over the senses), *dhih* (intellect), *vidya* (knowledge), *satyam* (truth) and *akrodhah* (absence of anger).

These principles are part of the eternal and Universal Truths that apply equally to all living entities regardless of class, caste, nationality, gender or any other temporary qualifications.

4

Explanations of the Essential Vedic Principles

PRINCIPLE 1—THE VEDIC TRADITION IS A WAY OF LIFE

The Vedic tradition or Hinduism is more than a religion, but a way of life, a complete philosophy for the foundation and direction for one's existence.

Many people are accustomed to a religion that has a certain set of beliefs or values that are the basis of one's spiritual view. What else one does beyond these core beliefs to figure out how to live has to come from some other source, or further explanations from the local priests and pastors. Often, the key values of a particular religion take on the form of this "ism" or that "ism", such as Mohammedism, Buddhism, Hinduism, Judaism, Shintoism, or Christianity, etc. But Hinduism is not merely another "ism" or belief system. It is not a set of rules you merely believe in, and then your spiritual search or experience grows no farther.

The Vedic tradition is a constant source of improvement and guidance, to propel the individual for searching and gaining more experience and insight, and to acquire increasingly deeper connections with the Divine. Thus, it is more a way of life for a continued process of growth and improvement than a religion or belief system.

Furthermore, it offers information and knowledge on all aspects of life, such as in the field of health in Ayurveda. Ayurveda is an important part of the Vedic system for analyzing one's body type and how to holistically live, eat, exercise and maintain the body for maximum health and benefit. This is part of the Dharmic way of life. This is only one indication of how the Vedic tradition is not simply a religion to follow but a process of living, a way of life to reach one's highest potential and spiritual consciousness.

PRINCIPLE 2—THE UNIVERSAL TRUTHS ARE FOR EVERYONE

It is based on Universal Spiritual Truths that can be applied to anyone at any-time.

As we are all spiritual beings in various kinds of material bodies, essential spiritual principles are thus applicable to all of us. And this is the primary focus of the Vedic or Dharmic way of life. The Vedic system is meant for helping us awaken to our real identity and then to act according to those revelations and realizations. In this way, the Vedic system is based on the Spiritual Truths that are applicable to everyone, in any location, in any time of the past, present or future. The spiritual strata does not change, it is eternal. The material energy, however, is in constant change, but the spiritual energy, of which we are a part as spiritual entities, is always the same. And Vedic knowledge is the essence of such Universal Spiritual Truths which explain our real, transcendental nature and identity.

PRINCIPLE 3—HINDUISM'S CORRECT NAME IS SANATANA-DHARMA

It is called Sanatana-dharma, the eternal nature of the soul.

It is generally accepted that it was the Persians who invaded India during the 6th century B.C. who gave the name "Hindu" for a society of people who lived in a certain region of India near the Sindhu river, later known as the Indus river. In Persian, the letter H and S are pronounced almost the same, so they mistook the S in the word Sindhu as H and then started calling the people Hindus and their religion as Hinduism. Thus, the name is actually a misnomer since there are many schools of thought and views of God within the umbrella term of Hinduism, each with its own specific name, such as Vaishnavas, Shaivites, Shaktas, Brahmanadis, etc.

Dr. Radhakrishnan has also observed about the name Hindu: "The Hindu civilization is so called since its original founders or earliest followers occupied the territory drained by the Sindhu (the Indus) river system corresponding to the North West Frontier Province and the Punjab. This is recorded in the *Rig Veda*, the oldest of the *Vedas*, the Hindu scripture which gives their name to this period of Indian history. The people on the Indian side of the Sindhu were called Hindu by the Persian and the later western invaders." This indicates that the name is not based on religion or theocracy, but is merely a name based on the particular locality of a people. This could also mean that numerous people, even tribals of India, Dravidians, or even the Vedic Aryans are all Hindus. Again, in this way, Hinduism can accommodate different communities, rites, various gods and practices.

Other originations of the word *Hindu* may be given, but they all essentially show that it was a name indicating a locality of a society, and it had nothing to do with the religion, philosophy, or way of life of the people. This is why some followers of Sanatana-dharma or Vedic culture, including various gurus, do not care to use the name Hindu to describe their spiritual path.

The more correct term for the Vedic process is the Sanskrit term *Sanatana-dharma*. This name means a path and a realization. Sanatana-dharma means the eternal nature of the living being. Just as the *dharma* of sugar is sweetness, and the *dharma* of fire is to burn and give warmth, the spiritual being also has a *dharma*. That *dharma* is to serve and love, and that love ultimately is meant to be the spiritual relationship between the living being and God and all other living entities. When that love and spiritual realization is attained, then the living being regains his natural Divinity. To attain this stage, one can follow the path of *dharma*. Thus, *dharma* is also a code of conduct. This, however, is not a dogma or forced standard, but it is a natural training that brings people to a higher level of consideration and consciousness. Thus, the whole of society can develop in this refined manner to a higher level of awareness and understanding of our connection with each other, with nature, and with God. This is why some followers of Sanatana-dharma call themselves Dharmists or Dharmis.

The *Manu-samhita* recommends the following characteristics to be developed for one who follows the Dharma. These include fortitude, forgiveness, self control, non-envy, purity, sense control, the ability to discriminate between good and evil, learning, truthfulness, and absence of anger. In this way we can understand that the moral and ethical principles of Sanatana-Dharma are universal and applicable to all everywhere. Everyone can develop the principles and virtues in their personal life, and society as a whole will be uplifted to higher levels of joy and peace. So we can imagine how much nicer the world could be if everyone developed these qualities. Therefore, Sanatana-dharma is also the path to attain our natural spiritual qualities.

Dharma also means the natural laws that sustain and hold together the whole universe. So *dharma* is also that which brings harmony and unity, because that is how the universe, along with society in general, is maintained and preserved. In this way, Sanatana-dharma is also the path that allows the individual to realize his or her spiritual position and true identity, and also brings the ultimate stage of harmony and balance to each person, to society, and to the whole planet. This is the Vedic process. It is thus a Universal Truth in that it can be applied anywhere in the universe and at any time in history, to any people or culture, and it will produce the same results for all. This brings us to our next point.

PRINCIPLE 4—THE VEDIC UNDERSTANDING OF GOD

It recognizes that there is one Supreme Being with no beginning or end, the all in all, the unlimited Absolute Truth, which can expand into many forms.

According to the Vedic understanding, there is only one God but there are three MAIN aspects of this Absolute Truth, namely Brahman, Paramatma and Bhagavan. One must understand all three aspects to get a full view of the Supreme Truth. Brahman is the formless but all-pervasive force and energy of God. It is the impersonal, non-dual aspect, or great white light of the Brahman effulgence. It is composed of innumerable souls which have merged into it, and is also the great rays or brilliance that emanate from the body of the Supreme Personality.

Paramatma is the form of the Lord as the Supersoul, the localized aspect of God. He is the Lord in the heart of every living being, and also the center of every molecule. It is He that witnesses all that we do, and even guides us when we surrender to His will. It is He that gives the ability in man, and motivates us as a conscience or guiding voice in our spiritual quest.

Then there is the Bhagavan aspect of God, which is God as the Supreme Being or Personality. After studying all the major Vedic texts, as also established by Lord Brahma who did this, they ultimately point to Lord Krishna and His expansion of Lord Vishnu as the main forms of the Supreme Being. It is these forms from which expand all other forms or *avataras* of God which appear for particular pastimes or purposes, all to show the various glories of God.

It is the Lord's personal form of Krishna with whom we can interact with and develop a truly loving relationship. Everyone knows that the highest happiness that we can find is that which exists in a loving relationship with someone. God is also the Supreme Lover, in whom we can find the highest happiness in a spiritual relationship. The spiritual world is meant for those who have purely desired a deep spiritual and loving relationship with God. For those who want something else, other realms are there so they can find such things, such as this material realm. Thus, the spiritual worlds are protected from any disturbances from the living beings who are not yet qualified for attaining the privilege of having a personal loving relationship in the spiritual domain.

The point is that to understand God completely, a person should understand all three aspects of God, namely Brahman, Paramatma and Bhagavan. It is not enough to comprehend only one aspect of God and think that God does not have the other facets, or to view God as only personal or impersonal. Sometimes a person who thinks that God ultimately has no form will disregard the Bhagavan aspect, or even think that it is elementary and for simple minded people. Such impersonalists may think that the personal form of God is a product of *maya*, the illusory energy, as if God cannot descend into the material world in His personal form. However, Lord Krishna clearly explains throughout the *Bhagavad-gita* that He is the controller of the illusory energy and that He is the Supreme Being who appears in His own personal form and of His own accord. Nonetheless, *mayavadis* are those who are convinced that the highest reality is but the formless Brahman and all other forms of God are merely temporary manifestations that are dependent on the material energy. But that is not correct.

There are also those who understand only the Bhagavan or personal form of God and who will think that impersonalists, or those focusing only on the Brahman aspect, have no proper understanding of God. Or that impersonalists will not accept the Lord's personal expansions and interactions with His devotees as real, since the Brahman is only an all-pervading and inactive force or energy. But actually it is said that until we understand all three of these basic features of God, our understanding of Him will never be complete. So we need to see how all three aspects of God are connected, and that by studying all three of these characteristics will provide us with a complete understanding of all the potentials of the Supreme Being.

It is further explained that God is also known as *sat-chit-ananda-vigraha*, or the complete form of eternity, all knowledge and supreme bliss. The first characteristic of *sat* is that God is eternal. He is the beginning, middle and end of everything. The *Vedanta Sutras* say that the Absolute Truth is He from whom all else exists. As Brahman, the all-pervasive spiritual energy, the Lord is omnipresent, consisting of both the finite and infinite realms of existence. God is beyond all materialistic forms of consideration and logic, thus God cannot be completely understood by our finite minds. However, God can and does reveal His characteristics so that the sincere devotee becomes eligible to understand the Lord. Thus, by one's servitude mentality, the Infinite becomes submissive to the sincere infinitesimal spirit soul.

By the *chit* characteristic, God is the one supreme consciousness, meaning full of knowledge and awareness of all. He knows everything that can and cannot be known. By such knowledge, the Lord maintains complete control over the creation and can alter its progress and development as He sees fit. He knows every consequence of every action that may take place. Thus, He is aware of every aspect of both the material and spiritual domains.

The *ananda* quality means the Lord is the form of the ultimate and complete bliss. We are all looking for knowledge, eternity, happiness, etc., and the Lord is the complete possessor of all such qualities. Thus, what we are looking for in completion is God. This *ananda* or bliss is beyond all material forms of happiness or pleasures. This bliss is based on the ultimate spiritual loving relationships and reciprocations for which we are always hankering. It is natural for the living entity to look for love because that love is the nature of the soul. And the source of all such deep and reciprocal love is the ultimate lover, God. But this is not physical or sensual love. It is beyond all such limitations and considerations. It is beyond the imagination. It is pure and unadulterated spiritual bliss. This is at first entered by the worship we offer to God. This is the means of connecting to God and that ever-increasing loving sentiment and reciprocation that we are looking for. It is infinite love beyond measure.

This, of course, is only the shortest of explanations on the characteristics of God. But that is the ultimate *vigraha* or form of God as *sat-chit-ananda-vigraha*: The eternal, all-knowing, ever-expanding blissful form of the personality of God.

PRINCIPLE 5—ALL EXISTENCE IS PART OF THE ONE GREAT TRUTH

All life is supported by and is part of the one great Truth, known as Brahman, eternal, fully conscious and joyful. This Supreme, eternal consciousness is transcendental and simultaneously manifests its true nature as both a personal deity and impersonal energy, as well as both male and female forms.

In the Vedic tradition the great *rishis* and masters have realized the eternal and all-pervading nature of the spiritual energy. This aspect is called the Brahman, the impersonal, omnipotent and omnipresent energy of God. The basis of everything is this eternal spiritual energy. However, the Supreme is also a personal being and deity, and appears as both male and female, such as in the case of Lakshmi-Vishnu, or Radha-Krishna, etc. God as a person exhibits His pastimes and characteristics when He descends as an *avatara*, and who also listens to prayers and reciprocates with the emotional and loving exchanges of His devotees. Those who are devoted can absorb themselves in such pastimes of the Divine and thus exhibit and increase their loving devotion to the Supreme, who puts on such displays to show His or Her personality, character, beauty, all for the pleasure of the devotees.

PRINCIPLE 6—THE AVATARAS OF GOD

The Divine Intelligence which supports all existence can and has appeared throughout history in the form of personal manifestations (*avataras*) within the realm of matter, and even in the sound vibration of scriptures (the Vedic literature).

An *avatara* is a descension of one of the forms of the Lord. Whenever God descends to earth in any form, then He is an *avatara*. There are numerous forms of God who descend into the material manifestation from the spiritual worlds to carry out and display particular pastimes or maintain the material creation, as well as attract the conditioned souls to return to the spiritual domain. By His causeless mercy the Lord appears in this world to raise up all beings to increasingly higher and higher levels of consciousness and to attract them to return back to the spiritual domain.

The ten most important *avataras* of Vishnu include Matsya (fish), Kurma (tortoise), Varaha (boar), Narasimha (man-lion), Vamana (dwarf), Parashurama (the warrior with an axe), Rama (the perfect king), Krishna (God of love), Buddha, and Kalki (God on the white horse). The Kalki *avatara* is yet to come. Hindus believe that the Kalki *avatara* will come in the future at the end of this age of Kali-Yuga and bring back the refined age of Satya-Yuga, the Golden Age.

Each *avatara* has a definite purpose and is described in the Vedic texts. Lord Vishnu came as a Matsya (fish) to save Sage Manu from the floods that covered the Earth and to recover the *Vedas* from a demon's hands. After that the Devas (gods of heaven) discovered that the divine nectar of immortality had been lost and it was at the bottom of the sea. Lord Vishnu helped in its recovery by becoming a Kurma (tortoise) to support a huge mountain on His back that was used as a churning rod to remake the nectar. Lord Vishnu took the Avatar of Varaha (boar) to kill a demon named Hiranyaksha, who dragged the Earth to the bottom of the universal Garbhodaka ocean. Lord Vishnu, after killing the demon, then brought the Earth back from the bottom of that ocean. After the death of Hiranyaksha, his twin-brother Hiranyakasipu became the king of demons. He made everyone treat him as God. Since Hiranyakasipu had received a boon from Lord Brahma that he could not be killed by either a man or an animal, Lord Vishnu took the form of a Narasimha (man-lion) and killed him. Lord Vishnu came as Vamana (the dwarf) to get rid of the pride of the demon-king Mahabali. Unlike any other demon, Mahabali was a very good king. During the reign of Mahabali, the world was like heaven and everyone was praising him in the three worlds. Lord Vishnu came down as Vamana and made Mahabali promise Him an area of land which He could cover in three steps. Mahabali agreed. Then Vamana immediately became a giant and took two steps that covered all the three worlds. His second step even punctured the covering of the universal shell and let in a drop of the spiritual Karana Ocean, which fell through the heavens and onto the Earth and became the Ganges River. He did not have a place to put his third step so Mahabali requested him to place his third step on his head. Then Vamana pushed Mahabali to the third world known as Patala. People in Kerala still celebrate the reign of Mahabali by a festival named Onam. Lord Vishnu also came as Parashurama (the warrior with an axe) to save the world from the tyranny of the evil Kshatriya kings. Then He came as Rama, to annihilate Ravana, the demon king of Lanka, as described in the *Ramayana*, and to show the example of an ideal king. The incarnation of Lord Vishnu as Krishna is the most popular *avatara* of all. There are many pastime stories of Lord Krishna. Hindus also consider the Buddha as an *avatara*. Kalki (who rides on a white horse) is an *avatara* yet to come to restore the Earth's purity. You should read *Srimad-Bhagavata* to get all details of these *avataras*.

With other incarnations of Lord Vishnu, according to the *Bhagavata Purana*, the main *avataras* number twenty-two. They consist of the ten incarnations already described and 12 more as follows: 1. Sanat Kumara and his three brothers; 2. Sage Narada (exponent of Bhakti and the Vaishnava Tantras): 3. Saints Nara and Narayana; 4. Sage Kapila (founder of the Samkhya System); 5. Dattatreya (the greatest magician who restored Vedic rites); 6. Yajna (Lord Vishnu as identified as the sacrificial rituals); 7. Rishabha (founder of the pre-Aryan Jain philosophy); 8. King Prithu; 9. Dhanvatari, the founder of Ayurveda (he came from the ocean of milk, holding the divine elixir, Amrith); 10. Balarama (brother of Lord Krishna and an embodiment of virtues); 11. Sage Veda Vyasa (author of the *Vedas*, *Vedanta Sutras*, *Mahabharata*, the *Bhagavatam* and other Vedic literature); and 12. Mohini (the Lord's feminine incarnation) who deprived the demons of the divine elixir, Amrith. There are still more *avataras* of Lord Vishnu which are not mentioned in the list above.

PRINCIPLE 7—THE SUPREME IS FOUND IN THE SPIRITUAL DIMENSION AND AS THE SUPERSOUL

That Supreme Being is found in the spiritual dimension but also lives in the heart of all living beings.

The Vedic texts and the experienced *acharyas* relate that besides being all-pervading through the Brahman, the Supreme also exists in the spiritual world, which has its own eternal atmosphere. Therein the spiritual sky are the Vaikuntha planets where the innumerable forms of Lord Vishnu reside, as well as the huge lotus-like realm of Goloka, Lord Krishna's personal abode.

Besides this, the Lord expands into the innumerable forms of the Paramatma, which is the Supreme's expansion as the localized aspect of the Supersoul in the heart of every living being. Thus the Lord is always very close to the living being, who merely has to awaken to this relationship between them.

PRINCIPLE 8—WE ARE ALL ETERNAL

The Vedic tradition recognizes that the individual soul is eternal, beyond the limitations of the body, and that one soul is no different than another.

The Vedic texts, such as the *Upanishads* and the *Bhagavad-gita*, provide complete explanations of the eternal nature of the soul, which is the real identity of every living being. The material bodies may display so many differences between one and another, but within each body is a soul. Each soul is essentially similar in its spiritual characteristics. So in this way, we are all the same.

The symptom of the soul is the consciousness of each living being. Without the soul there is no life in the material body. The soul is never subjected to death or misery, or any influence of the material energy like the body is. It is completely spiritual and eternal. The goal of human life is to reawaken our spiritual awareness of our real identity as the soul, which is completely free from material limitations. Thus, the more Self-realized we become, the more we regain our spiritual constitutional position and the happier we will be.

PRINCIPLE 9—THE SOUL UNDERGOES REINCARNATION

The soul incarnates through different forms (called *samsara* or reincarnation) until it reaches liberation (*moksha*) from the repetition of birth and death, and attains its natural position in the spiritual domain.

Hindus or Dharmists, along with most every other religion, believe in life after death. According to the Vedic philosophy, the body alone dies, the soul within is eternal and thus never dies. The process of reincarnation means that the soul takes another birth in a material body to continue with material experiences or the pursuit of material desires. Thoughts and desires create a level of consciousness for the individual. This consciousness at the time of death is what determines a person's next life. Then, after death, a person is drawn toward a new body and set of circumstances that are most suitable for that person's level of desires and thinking.

There has been an increasing number of books written by professionals that document the stories of those who have remembered their past lives, especially children who have no ulterior reason to mention their memories about previous lives. Yet, the evidence these researchers have provided has shown that reincarnation and living multiple lifetimes is a fact and has been going on indefinitely.

The path the soul takes into another birth is decided upon by past actions, which is known as karma. Due to the law of karma, an individual makes his or her own destiny. Karma is the universal principle based on the moralistic saying "As you sow, so shall you reap". The theory of karma is that every action has its opposite and equal reaction. As you do something, the intention and the act will come back to you. If you do something good, something good will come back. And if you commit a bad action upon others, that reaction will again come back to befall on you. Such karma can then accumulate so that it affects your future, either in this life or the next. Sometimes the actions that a person may commit will carry such serious karma that they will require many lifetimes to work out. At other times, the karma is simple enough that even in this life one will experience the good or bad effects. However, if one is too self-centered, or too sinful, then the results of such karma will take one into very dark places of existence, the likes of which some would call hell.

So as we look at ourselves, we may also say that our present life is the result of past karma, and our present actions will create our future circumstances. Thus, it is not that God brings punishment upon us, but as we reincarnate through life, by our own actions we create our own experiences, or lessons, rewards, and challenges that we need to go through to learn what we must in order to become a better person. Our karma is a matter of creating balance within us and in our actions. So in a sense you could say that all karma is good karma because it helps us work out what we must to be a more balanced being in all of our ways. Therefore, by understanding the law of karma we accept the responsibility of our own actions and take guard to be careful of what we do. This is an automatic principle when we are serious about any spiritual path.

So the actions of our former body do not die with the body. Past actions and the karma from them are attached to the subtle body and carry over from one physical life to the next. This is what determines the kind of body the soul takes in the next life and what situations of happiness or suffering will affect it. When an individual soul exhausts all its material desires and karmas, it is free to enter into the spiritual domain, in which case Hindus say that the soul has attained *moksha* or liberation.

How many lifetimes we spend in this universe is up to us. The Vedic literature, especially the *Bhagavad-gita*, very clearly says that one can attain liberation in one life, provided one surrenders his will to the will of God. This is done by understanding and following the Lord's instructions. This sort of surrender allows one to spiritualize his or her consciousness, in which case all material desires become insignificant and then eliminated. And without any material desires to fulfill, there is no further need to take birth in another material body. The point is, you cannot fulfill material desires without a material body. But when one purifies himself through spiritual practice, one can become free from such desires and become eligible for liberation into the spiritual domain. Lord Krishna says: "Those who surrender all actions to Me and regard Me as the supreme goal and worship Me with whole hearted devotion, I will deliver them from repeated births and deaths." In another verse, Lord Krishna says: "Abandon all varieties of religion and just surrender unto Me. I shall deliver you from all sinful reaction. Do not fear." (*Bg.*18.66) Thus, our eagerness to surrender to God will certainly diminish the need for further rounds of birth and death in a material body in this cosmic manifestation. In fact, we can become liberated in this one life if we are serious and sincere.

According to Vedic knowledge, it is not necessarily so that a human will always reincarnate as a human being. If a man exhibits beastly character throughout his life, the low consciousness that he develops will see to it that he reincarnates as a beast. His consciousness will take him downward to the appropriate kind of body. A glutton may take birth as a pig or another lower form of life. The *Vedas* mention 8.4 million species of life, right from an amoeba up to human beings and demigods. A living being can take any of these life-forms. Sometimes the soul will also remain in a standstill state for long periods of time, existing in the subtle realm without taking any body at all. However, the soul can work out its karma through bodily existence either gross or subtle only if it takes a body. But it can become free of karma through spiritual practice, called *sadhana*. So for attaining liberation, the soul is bound to reincarnate until it attains spiritual perfection.

Lord Krishna has explained in the *Bhagavad-gita* that whatever one thinks of during the time of death, one will attain that in the next life. So the whole process of religion or spiritual practice is to raise one's consciousness and spiritually purify it so that we can enter the spiritual dimension after death. But a man who has beastly ideas and desires throughout his life is unlikely to think of God at the time of death. He will likely take his beastly thoughts and desires into the next life, which will propel him to his next form of existence. Only God-fearing people can think of God at the time of death; others will think of a multitude of things but not about God. And that is what propels one towards the next appropriate body which will accommodate that consciousness.

PRINCIPLE 10—THE GOAL OF THE VEDIC PROCESS

The ultimate purpose of human life is to shed all attachments to matter and attain *moksha* (liberation from material existence) and return to the transcendental realm which is not only our true nature, but also our real home.

There are both long term and short term goals in the Vedic process.

The Short-Term Goal is to find happiness. This is generally done through the process of *kama* (pleasure or material and sensual happiness), *artha* (worldly success and material possessions), *dharma* (religious duty) and *moksha* (liberation from material existence). We find happiness through *dharma* or religious duty in which we act and pray to God or the demigods for the facility that we need to be comfortable and happy in life. Then *artha* is the means of being happy through economic development by learning a career, trade, or simply a means of earning an income. Then we have the money to buy or do what gives us pleasure. Next is *kama*, or the means of sensual pleasure and satisfaction, which is usually attained by having a nice wife or husband in which we can enjoy their company and have children in family life. Finally, after we have experienced most everything we can in this life, we focus our religious concerns more seriously so that we may attain *moksha*, or liberation from material existence altogether.

Most people will first focus on finding material and physical happiness. We all need a certain amount of *kama* or happiness and pleasure to be content and remain motivated to keep living, but physical and mental pleasure itself is not enough to satisfy the real and deeper nature of humanity. Sooner or later we want to experience a wider range of happiness and contentment.

So then we move on to *artha*, or the endeavor to be financially successful through a career, a trade or business so we can accumulate wealth and material goods. This may also include fame and power. This often involves the affect we can have on the lives of others, which brings its own sets of pleasures and expands one's greed. However, such endeavors and accomplishments are competitive in nature and cannot be shared without one's own property or money being reduced. Thus, the more power or money one has, the more worry goes into protecting and keeping it, which sometimes drives a person to extremes in worry and concern to keep and get more of what one has. We often see how this causes a person to feel unexplainably empty though having much in the way of material comforts. A Vedic saying sums the situation up appropriately when it says: "To try to extinguish the drive for riches with money is like trying to quench a fire by pouring ghee (clarified butter) on it", which only makes the fire increase. Therefore, such goals can easily become a serious distraction to the real goal of life, unless one is especially sober-minded and aware of the temporary nature of all such forms of material pleasure, happiness and financial success. Therefore, the Vedic path includes *dharma*.

Dharma includes the Vedic spiritual practices that make one's life complete. *Dharma* includes proper actions, duty and selfless service. *Dharma* also means to defend against *adharma* or those who wish to promote the ways opposed to *dharma*. Without *dharma*, one's life is basically wasted. All else will vanish with time and be forgotten, leaving a person with little else but the endeavor that was applied to accomplish one's goals.

Finally, if one's dharmic activities are sincere, serious and successful, there is *moksha*. *Moksha* is the real goal of life which is attained when one becomes spiritually Self-realized. *Moksha* means liberation from the continuous cycles of birth and death. What is the benefit of so many lifetimes that simply perpetuate one's karma to undergo more and more rounds of birth and death in this material world? Therefore, without *dharma* and then *moksha*, which is the ultimate freedom, one's life remains incomplete.

The higher goal is that by understanding our spiritual identity, we also become free from the day to day turmoil and hassles that many people take so seriously. Some people let such problems control their lives. Life is too short for that. Allowing such circumstantial difficulties to increase our stress and anxiety only decreases our duration of life.

Life is meant for being happy. But real happiness, which exists on the spiritual platform, is always steady and, in fact, is continually increasing according to one's spiritual advancement. Such persons who understand their spiritual identity and are self-satisfied and content within themselves find happiness everywhere. This is what the Vedic process tries to give everyone.

The *Chandogya Upanishad* (starting at 7.25.2) explains that he who perceives and understands this, loves the self, revels, rejoices, and delights in the self. Such a person is lord and master of the worlds because he has already attained all that he needs. He knows that he may be in this material world but is not of it. He is actually of the spiritual world and has regained his connection with it. Therefore, he looks at this world as if he were simply a tourist. He sees all the busy activities of people and society, the confusion, but he walks through it all unaffected. But those who think differently live in perishable worlds and have other mortal beings as their rulers. They are limited and controlled by their own material designations. But he who sees the soul of everyone, the spiritual identity beyond the body, does not see death, nor illness, nor pain; he who sees this sees everything and obtains everything everywhere. This certainly is the quality of those who have attained their own internal, self-sufficient happiness.

A similar verse is found in the *Katha Upanishad* (2.5.12-13) where it says that those who have realized their self and also see the Supreme Being residing within their heart and in all beings as the Superself, to them belongs eternal happiness and eternal peace, but not to others.

The original spiritual form of the living being is *sac-chit-ananda*: eternal, full of knowledge, and full of bliss, similar to the form of God, but the difference is that God is infinite and we are infinitesimal. The living being's spiritual form is never limited by the body or one's situation. The only limiting factor is the living being's consciousness or lack of spiritual awareness. When the living entity, after many births, finally regains his original spiritual consciousness, realizing he is not the body, he naturally feels very happy and jolly, being freed from the limited and temporary perspective one has while being controlled by the illusory, material energy. He also understands that this material world is not his real home, and it has nothing substantial to offer him since real pleasure and happiness actually come from within on the spiritual level. As stated in *Bhagavad-gita* by Lord Sri Krishna: "One who is thus transcendentally situated at once realizes the Supreme Brahman and becomes fully joyful. He never laments nor desires to have anything; he is equally disposed to every living entity. In that state he attains pure devotional service to Me." (*Bg.*18.54)

In this way, "The yogi whose mind is fixed on Me [Lord Sri Krishna] verily attains the highest happiness. By virtue of his identity with Brahman [the absolute spiritual nature], he is liberated; his mind is peaceful, his passions are quieted, and he is freed from sin. Steady in the Self, being freed from all material contamination, the yogi achieves the highest perfectional stage of happiness in touch with the Supreme Consciousness." (*Bg.*6.27-28)

"Such a liberated soul is not attracted to material sense pleasure or external objects but is always in trance, enjoying the pleasure within. In this way the self-realized person enjoys unlimited happiness, for he concentrates on the Supreme." (*Bg.*5.21)

This happiness, therefore, is the goal of all people, and is the highest level of happiness which is attained when one understands his or her true spiritual identity and becomes spiritually Self-realized.

The Long-Term Goal: The ultimate goal of the Vedic process is *moksha*, or liberation and the release from *samsara*, or the continuous cycles of birth and death, otherwise called reincarnation. This liberation is the position of the soul when it regains or reawakens its spiritual consciousness to the fullest extent. When one's consciousness is purified or completely spiritualized, and when the soul has regained its spiritual position and completely acts on that level, then there is no more need to take birth in a material body for the pursuit of material desires. One then enters back into the spiritual world, which is the natural home of the spirit soul, when the finite living entity returns to the Infinite.

The Vedic concept of salvation is different from that of the Christians. Hindu salvation is known as Self-realization and rising above and being freed from ignorance. In Vedic philosophy, salvation or liberation means that a person realizes that he is not the body, but the immortal soul (*Atman*) within. That is the reason why Hindu salvation is known as Self-Realization or realizing that one is the Immortal Self and not the perishable body. This realization is the means of rising above the illusion that keeps us from being free. Real freedom on the Vedic path is freedom from material and sensual desires. Such desire is the basis of what keeps us bound up in earthly existence and in *samsara*.

The Vedic system includes various processes in order to assist the living being to attain this freedom. According to the position and consciousness of the person, he or she may be interested in different processes, though some are more highly recommended in this present age than others. These may include the process of *Jnana* (knowledge), *Vijnana* (realized knowledge), Hatha-yoga (the practice of keeping the body in shape for ultimately pursuing spiritual consciousness), Yoga (the process for altering and uplifting the consciousness), and *Bhakti* (the process of devotion in which attaining the Grace of God is the main focus). Each one of these systems or divisions deserves its own description to fully understand them, some of which will be summarized later in this book.

So Vedic culture takes it for granted that there is more than one approach to understand different levels of spiritual Truth and attain liberation, and that these different approaches are not only compatible with each other, but are also complimentary. Thus, the disagreements that you find in most conventional and monotheistic religions, and the friction between the various sects that often develop, are not so much a part of the Vedic culture, even though individual preferences may exist.

This is also why, generally speaking, many Hindus will respect all religions. They may be initiated by a Vedic guru, devoutly practice yoga, attend the temple regularly, yet still go to see some Christian preacher, or Buddhist teacher, or even hear an Islamic Imam talk about God. They may do this with the idea of attaining new insights, yet still not consider themselves falling away from their own path or converting to a different religion. Yet, if a Christian or Muslim would do such a thing as participate in an alternative religion, or even a different sect from which they belong, they may be considered sinful and apostates, or at least hypocrites deserving of some punishment. But such narrow-mindedness hardly touches the person following the Vedic path.

PRINCIPLE 11—WE ARE SPIRITUAL BEINGS IN THE REALM OF MATTER

All living entities, both human and otherwise, are the same in their essential and divine spiritual being. All of them are parts of the eternal truth, and have appeared in this world to express their nature and also to gather experience in the realms of matter.

As we regain our awareness of our true spiritual nature and identity, we become more attentive to the fact that we are all parts of the eternal spiritual Truth that is the basis and reason of our existence. Though we are essentially spiritual beings, somehow we have entered material existence within one of the many physical forms in which we presently find ourselves. And we are now expressing ourselves in various ways, especially through our loving nature, such as love for our family, wife or husband, friends and society, etc. This loving propensity is the nature of the soul. But the ultimate objective for the soul is to enter into a loving relationship with God.

However, since many of us have not done that, we are gaining lessons in dealing with and experiencing what it is like to live in the material world and love various objects and beings that are all temporary. The material manifestation and all forms we see are but temporary creations, and thus all relations we have in this world as expressed through and with such ephemeral bodies are also temporary. From this we can learn the joys and sorrows of the transitory material existence. Yet through such lessons, we learn the importance of spiritual knowledge and of reawakening the awareness of our real identity. Then we also realize that transcendental to these material forms, on the spiritual platform, we are all the same in character, and all related to each other as parts of the divine spiritual Truth.

PRINCIPLE 12—WE ARE ONE UNIVERSAL FAMILY

For this reason, Vedic followers accept the premise of *Vasudhaiva Kutumbakam,* that all living beings in the universe comprise one family, and that as such all beings are spiritually equal and should be respected as members within that family of the Supreme.

If we can reach genuine spiritual understanding and awareness, we will see that we are all higher and above whatever temporary material designations we may have given ourselves. In materialistic consciousness we only see ourselves as the bodies we inhabit, which all appear different from one another. Thus, based on bodily identification we think we are all dissimilar. But with spiritual understanding and transcendental vision, we can see we are all creations of God, or sons and daughters of the same Supreme Father. This is how God sees us. And this is how all beings are a part of the one universal family under the Supreme Being. If we could all see each other in this way and respect one another in this manner, the world and our relations in society would drastically change most quickly for the better. This is why the followers of the Vedic tradition honor the phrase and concept of *Vasudhaiva Kutumbakam,* one universal family amongst all beings.

This attitude is shown by the use of the word *namaste* or *namaskar* when Hindus greet each other, which indicates respect to the God within you. Dharmists accept that everyone is part of God and a part of God's family. Thus, no one is eternally damned, nor are some a chosen people who have a special connection with God that others do not have. Nor are others damned for being "non-believers". We all have a connection with God and we all merely need to awaken that relationship. Until then we are all in various stages of forgetfulness or awakening of that relationship with God.

This is also why Hindus respect the good in other religions and cultures and ways to God, and do not divide the world between believers and non-believers, or the faithful and the infidels. Such divisions make no sense to a true Dharmist.

PRINCIPLE 13—SPIRITUAL PROGRESS DOES NOT DEPEND ON ONE'S BIRTH

Every person's capacity to spiritually progress depends upon their personal qualities, choices and abilities, and are not limited by the circumstances of one's color, caste, class or any other circumstance of birth or temporary material limitation or designations.

The Vedic system does not force everyone into one category or expect the same from each person when it comes to the process they may need for their spiritual development. It recognizes that the main factor in a person's spiritual development is their consciousness and what level of awareness a person is starting from. Everyone's consciousness is not the same, which means that each person may need a specific method or practice that is most suitable for their level of understanding.

Furthermore, the ability for one to make spiritual progress has nothing to do with one's race, social class or circumstances of birth. These are only material factors which do not implicate the soul in being able to attain spiritual consciousness. It all depends on one's education, training and sincerity to engage in spiritual practice to affect the person's consciousness in higher levels of perception. This is why everyone is allowed to participate in a particular method or certain aspect of the Vedic process and continue according to their own abilities. It is not like anyone is considered an infidel or eligible to be excommunicated as found in other religions simply for having a different standard or view of spiritual Truth. Thus, the Vedic system has something for everyone, and in whatever way a person participates, he or she can still be considered a part of the Dharmic family.

PRINCIPLE 14—RESPECT FOR INDIVIDUAL FREEDOM OF INQUIRY

The Vedic path is based on regaining our natural spiritual identity. To pursue this goal, all human beings have the eternal right to choose their personal form of spiritual practice, as well as the right to reject any form of religious activity, and that coercion, forced conversion or commercial inducement should never be used or tolerated to present, propagate or enforce one's spiritual beliefs on others.

It is for this reason, as stated above, that the Vedic culture is wonderfully catholic, elastic and even democratic. It provides the epitome of the individual's right for self-inquiry and spiritual pursuit. It is this reason that it also maintains a liberal amount of tolerance and unlimited freedom for one's own method of private worship. It is, after all, up to the individual to carry on with one's own spiritual progress. Everything else in the Vedic system is for a person's assistance. It is not meant for being a religious dogma or to stifle or control, though it does expect one to stay within the laws of the land and ride the high ground of morality and spiritual discipline.

It is also because of this tolerance and mutual respect that you find members of Hinduism, Islam, Christianity, Buddhism, and even Zoroastrianism, Jainism, Sikhism, and the Parsis all accepting the shelter of life in India. India also allows all of the various sects of Islam to exist, whereas no other Islamic nation provides for such freedom within its own religion.

It is merely the fanaticism that comes from the fundamental and monotheistic religions that have sparked the majority of violence that has been seen in India and throughout the world. It is also the ways of the various monotheistic religions and their conversion tactics that have encroached on the culture and land of the Hindus that have made Hindus view them with suspicion, and be less than welcoming in some areas of the country. It has made them to be more protective of their culture, taking up various means of defense that has been called communalism or saffronization by the so-called secular media. Yet, Hindus cannot be expected to humble themselves out of their own existence. Hindus make lousy terrorists, and they will not be such. But they also do not need to be the doormat of every other religion that wants another part of India.

So, if left to themselves, Hindus and the followers of Vedic culture will continue to be one of the largest shelters for the greatest number of diverse religious groups there can be. The Vedic Dharma will continue to be a most tolerant, liberal, and respectful system of spiritual development, without the usual violence and persecution toward "non-believers" that seems to be the attendant of so many other less tolerant, monotheistic religions. It is this inherent acceptance of the right of the individual to proceed in the spiritual quest that is most suitable for him or her that separates the Vedic process from most other religions on the planet.

PRINCIPLE 15—THE WONDER AND BEAUTY OF THE VEDIC PATH

The Vedic path offers personal freedom for one to make his or her own choice of how he or she wants to pursue their spiritual approach, and what level of the

Absolute Truth he or she wishes to understand. This is spiritual democracy and freedom from tyranny.

Hinduism is open, with open doors and open windows, meaning no closed minds. So it does not promote a supremacy of any particular point of view as the only way. It has respect for all ways to God, and different ways are provided within the Vedic context for different people, depending on what they need. This is a rare point to find in religion. The Vedic process allows for the utmost freedom of thoughts and actions in the system for understanding the Absolute Truth. Sanatana-dharma never forbids anyone to question its fundamentals. In other words, anyone can ask any question they want without feeling that it is overstepping or questioning the authority of the Vedic teachings. Whereas if you ask too many questions in other religions, you can be criticized or ostracized from the religion. That's what attracts many to Hinduism.

In Vedic culture, you may come across people engaged in simple acts of worship on one side, and on the other you will come across concepts parallel to Quantum Physics and Neil's Bohr Theory of nuclear structure and reactions. On one side there is the Advaita or nondual philosophy, and still on another side there is the Dvaita or dualist philosophy. Sanatana-dharma never banished anyone for inquiring into some aspect of God, or for accepting a particular Vedic text or scripture, or for not observing a particular ritual.

Mahatma Gandhi said that even atheists can call themselves Hindus. Voltaire in an Essay on Tolerance wrote: "I may disagree with what you say, but I will defend to the death, your right to say it." In the same way, Hinduism maintains this principle of individuality and freedom for investigating the way to reaching the Absolute Truth. The Vedic system not only allows but actually encourages one to seek truths from all sources.

Vedic Dharma has no problem facing any type of questions. In fact, most of the Vedic texts are structured around questions and answers of all kinds. It has answers for everything and covers a multitude of topics, as an analysis of the Vedic texts will reveal. It does not have to hide behind what may appear to be unquestionable spiritual dogmas. It absorbs new ideas like the use of technology and modern science, psychology, and so on. Within Vedic culture, you can think and argue on any subject.

PRINCIPLE 16—ALL LIFE IS PRECIOUS

Recognizing the value and sanctity of all forms of life, as well as the Eternal Divine Being that is their true Self, the Vedic principle is that we should therefore strive in every possible way to peacefully co-exist with all other species of living entities.

As a person progresses in understanding the real spiritual identity of all living beings and the nature of the soul, a person will realize how all life is precious, in whatever form it may appear. Thus, a person who follows Vedic Dharma will appreciate the living being in all species of life. He or she will also honor and respect the environment and nature that makes it possible for all living beings to exist, and try to work in harmony with nature for the welfare of the planet and all living beings that exist on it. In this way, everyone and all living beings can live as peacefully as possible, and not at the expense or the suffering of others. Dharmists or Hindus acknowledge the sacredness of all life, including plants, trees, fish, fowl, insects, reptiles, animals and creatures of all kinds. Hindus also have a high consideration for the environment, knowing that it is the means of life for all beings. After all it is God's creation and God's environment, and we are dependent on it. For this reason, Dharmists also live mostly on the easy and healthy diet of vegetables, fruits and grains without the need to consume meat, which requires the painful slaughter of other beings simply to provide pleasure to the tongue and selfish satisfaction for the palate.

Proper nutrition and tasty dishes can be easily made from vegetables and fruits and non-meat ingredients. Thus, a Dharmist does not live by the pain and suffering of others, and lives peacefully with all species of life, knowing they are also spirit souls and parts of God though in other forms of existence.

PRINCIPLE 17—THE LAW OF KARMA

The soul undergoes it's own karma, the law of cause and effect, by which each person creates his own destiny based on his thought, words and deeds. The soul undergoes this karma in the rounds of reincarnation. All beings that exist are subject to and will ultimately be held accountable to the Laws of Nature, which are of Divine Origin.

The understanding of reincarnation is not complete without understanding the law of karma. So followers of Sanatana-dharma also accept the Biblical concept "Whatever a man soweth, that shall he reap." The doctrine of karma has been elaborated since the days of the *Rig-Veda* and it is very well explained in the *Brihadaranyaka Upanishad*. Every action and every thought has a reaction. That is the basis of karmic law. This is also the second law of thermodynamics: that every action has an opposite and equal reaction. On the universal level this is the law of karma. Applying the law of karma to individual development means that every thought and every action produces a reaction of some kind that will manifest in our lives. It is weighed on the scale of eternal justice. The law of karma is one of cause and effect. Nobody can escape from any karmic debt since it follows you throughout the universe.

So if you act piously and righteously, such action produces good or heavenly reactions. If you act cruelly, such acts produce bad or even hellish reactions, or reversals in life. So whatever we do in this life is felt in the form of good or bad reactions later in this or the next life. In the same way, our present life is based on a combination of the good or bad reactions from what we have done in previous lives. So the idea is to become free from such reactions, no matter whether they be good or bad so we can become free from taking any more births in this world. Then, with a spiritualized consciousness, we can reach the spiritual domain.

According to Vedic knowledge, the body alone dies, the soul never dies. But past actions are attached to the soul and they decide the path of the soul's travel. So if you are born rich or poor, it is because of your actions in a previous life. If you are born with disease, that also is the result of your past actions done in previous lives. After death, the soul carries a heavy load of karma and seeks an ideal body to be born in again. If you had lived as an evil individual in your last life, then the soul will take birth in a home where people may be leading evil lives. You will be forced to endure the consequences of your nefarious activities. However, if you had lived a pious life, then you will be reborn in an ideal home where both parents will be pious and happy. On the other hand, if you are born in a good and rich family because of your pious acts from a previous life, yet all you do is engage in selfish or cruel activities in this life, then you will simply use up all your good karma and pave the way to a lower birth in your next life.

According to Vedic understanding, the soul continues this journey with its load of karma from one life to another until it exhausts all karma by either undergoing the appropriate amount of pain or pleasure in the body, or by becoming purified through spiritual practice. The different methods of *sadhana* or God-realization provide easy ways to put an end to this drama of the continuous ups and downs in the body that you are given according to one's karma.

One point to consider is that God will never punish us. He does not have to. God has created man near to perfection and has given him the "Free will" to decide what he or she wants to do. God never interferes in our decisions. There is no such thing as being cursed or punished by God. God does not have to do that. He is always trying to call us home to the spiritual worlds. It is we ourselves who make our lives miserable or happy. We do that to ourselves by our own actions and the resulting reactions. Even when we suffer from heavy storms, tornadoes, earthquakes, hurricanes, and so on, it is merely the environment reflecting the general mass consciousness of the people who inhabit the planet. Even in the *Bhagavad-gita*, Lord Krishna never tried to influence Arjuna's free will. Lord Krishna, like an adviser, only discussed with Arjuna (his disciple) the various options he could take in his life and then let him make his own decision. So the condition of our lives and even of the planet is merely a reflection of the consciousness of the people who inhabit it. And it is simply one's ignorance to say that something is the "Revenge of God".

PRINCIPLE 18—THE MATERIAL MANIFESTATION IS DESIGNED AND CREATED

Material nature was designed and created, and is maintained and finally destroyed, by the purposeful actions of an all-pervading Divine Intelligence. The realms of matter are endlessly cyclic in nature. They are created, maintained for some time, annihilated and then begun again.

This is the essential understanding of how the material creation has a beginning, middle and end. It is created and goes through a variety of cycles in its existence, and then is finally annihilated, only to be created again. This is all arranged and under the guidance of a Divine Intelligence and not merely by chance circumstances. God is the ultimate creator of the universe and does so by His own self-sufficient power. He sustains the universe through His potencies and agents, and after its purpose is over withdraws it back into Himself. Thus, the creation and annihilation of the cosmic manifestation is a cyclic process. In this way, everything has a purpose, and we are a part of that objective. So our own lives have reason and purpose for our existence. Life is not an accident.

PRINCIPLE 19—HINDUS WORSHIP MANY GODS?

The processes and functions of material Nature are assisted by Divine Helpers (*devas*) who, though invisible to us, are real and with whom we live in a reciprocal relationship of mutual responsibility.

Sometimes we hear it said that in Hinduism or Vedic culture there are millions of gods, even as many as 33 million. Yet, if we properly analyze the situation, we will understand that there is but one Supreme Being who expands into many aspects or many *avataras*, and who also has many agents or demigods who may represent Him and assist in managing the creation and the natural forces within it. These demigods are great beings who rose to lofty positions by their own pious activities and who have been empowered to manage various aspects of the universe, and to facilitate humanity with the material commodities and blessings that they may need. And, like anyone else, if they are properly approached with prayer or worship, they may help facilitate the person by granting certain wishes that may be within the jurisdiction of that particular demigod. Thus, it is not uncommon to find Hindus petitioning or worshiping some of these gods for benefits, both material and spiritual. It should be noted, however, that such beings or demigods are like the officers of government who exercise the powers that have been delegated to them by higher authorities. The ultimate higher authority is, of course, the Supreme Being.

According to the *Vedas*, the demigods are not imaginary or mythological beings, but are agents of the Supreme Will to help administer different features of the universal affairs. They also represent and control various powers of nature. Thus, they manifest in the physical, subtle or psychic levels of existence both from within us and without. A transcendentalist sees that behind every aspect of nature is a personality. For example, when you walk into a big factory, you see so many workers and all that they are doing. You may initially think that these workers are the reason for whatever goes on in the factory. However, more important than the workers are the foremen, then the managers, and then the executives. Finally, a chief executive officer or president of the company is the most important of all. Without him there may not even be a company. You may not see the president right away, but his influence is everywhere since all the workers are engaging in projects according to his decisions. The managers and foremen act as his authorized agents to keep things moving accordingly. The numerous demigods act in the same way concerning the functions of nature. That's why it is sometimes said there are 33 million different gods in Hinduism. Actually, there may be many aspects of God, and many beings who are demigods, but there is only one Supreme God, or one Absolute Truth.

PRINCIPLES 20 & 21—THE DIVINITY OF THE VEDIC TEXTS AND SANSKRIT

The Vedic culture has a complete library of ancient texts known as the Vedic literature that explain these truths and the reasons for the tradition.

This Vedic literature is considered to be non-ordinary books that are the basis of the Vedic system. Some of these have been given or spoken by God, and others were composed by sages in their deepest super conscious state in which they were able to give revelations of Universal Truths while in meditation on the Supreme.

The Vedic literature provides the spiritual knowledge and instructions for assisting all living beings in their material and spiritual development and understanding. The Vedic library does not only contain the means for understanding and practicing the methods that can elevate one's consciousness to perceiving the spiritual dimension, but it also deals with many other topics to guide humanity for the best means of utilizing human existence for the highest purpose.

The Vedic texts are written in Sanskrit. Sanskrit, which literally means "cultured or refined", is the classical language of India and is the oldest and the most systematic language in the world. The various Sanskrit mantras that are used in the prayers and rituals in the Vedic system of worship are constructed in a particular formula to invoke special potencies. When they are chanted with the proper intonations, they exert a purifying and uplifting effect on those who listen, and also charge the atmosphere with its power.

Forbes Magazine, (July, 1987) wrote: "Sanskrit is the mother of all the European languages and is the most suitable language for the computer software." Furthermore, it is older than Hebrew or Latin. According to the PBS video "The Story of English" the first words in the English language came from Sanskrit. The word "mother" came from the Sanskrit word "mata", and "father" came from the Sanskrit word "pita". Believe it or not the word "geometry" came from a Sanskrit word called "Gyaamiti" meaning "measuring the earth". The word "trigonometry" came from the Sanskrit word "trikonamiti", which means "measuring triangular forms". With a little more research a person can find numerous other similarities and connections between Sanskrit and many other languages.

PRINCIPLES 22 & 23—WHAT ARE THE VEDIC TEXTS

The Vedic literature provides the spiritual knowledge and instructions for assisting all living beings in their material and spiritual development and understanding.

This Vedic literature, including, among other texts, the *Rig, Sama, Yajur* and *Atharva Vedas,* the *Upa-Vedas, Vedangas, Shadarshanas, Upanishads,* the *Vedanta-Sutras, Yoga Sutras, Agamas,* the *Ramayana,* the *Mahabharata* and *Bhagavad-gita,* and all Puranic literature and the practices congruent with them, contain the spiritual basis of the Hindu/Sanatana-dharma spiritual culture.

To elaborate more clearly on what are the Vedic texts, they started with the *Shruti*. *Shruti* literally means "That which is heard". For long periods of time there was no Vedic literature. It was a vocal or oral tradition, and passed down accordingly. The *Vedas* and *Upanishads* were in *Shruti* form for a long period of time. In fact, the word *Upanishad* means "Upa (near), Ni (down), Shad (sit)." This means that the teachings of the *Upanishads* are conveyed from guru to disciple, when the disciple sits very close at the feet of the guru.

The very first of the sacred books of Vedic culture, in fact the oldest books on earth, are called the *Vedas*. The word *Veda* means knowledge. The word *Veda* came from the root word *vid* meaning "to know". The *Vedas* are the very first scriptures of Vedic culture, which was not called Hinduism at the time. *Vedas*, as described by the scriptures, were given by God. There are four Vedic *samhitas*, which are the *Rig-Veda, Sama-Veda, Atharva-Veda,* and *Yajur-Veda.* The Sanskrit word *samhita* means "put together". They contain wisdom that has been assembled to teach men the highest aspects of truths which can lead them to higher levels of existence, as well as to God. The *Vedas* also discuss rituals and ceremonies to attain Self-realization as well as wisdom that deals with many other aspects of life. These four *samhitas* primarily contain the basic texts of hymns, formulas and chants to the various Vedic deities.

To briefly described them, the *Rig-Veda*—Veda of Praise—contains 10,522 verses in 1,017 hymns in ten books called *mandalas.* The *Rig-Veda* is the oldest book in the world. The *Rig-Veda* was around for many years before it was finally compiled in written form. According to Bal Gangadhar Tilak and the Vedic tradition, it was written around 5000 BC. The *Rig-Veda* is older than Gilgamesh (2500 B.C.) and the Old Testament.

In the *Rig-Veda* there are 100 hymns addressed to Soma; 250 addressed to Indra; 200 hymns addressed to Agni; and many addressed to Surya. Few others are addressed to the Ushas, Aditi, Saraswati, Varuna, and the Asvins. Lord Vishnu is not addressed so often therein because the *Vedas* focused more on appeasing the demigods for blessings to attain material facility rather than liberation.

The *Yajur-Veda*, which is essentially the *Veda* of liturgy, contains some 3988 verses dealing with rules and regulations for conducting rituals and also offers various levels of wisdom and advice. It is based on the *Rig-Veda* and consists of prose as well as verse. This *Veda* is indeed a priestly handbook, even describing the details of how to make an alter.

The *Sama-Veda*, the *Veda* of chants, offers knowledge of music in 1549 verses. *Sama* means "melody". The classical Indian music originated from this *Veda*.

This *Veda* is also connected with the *Rig-Veda*. To some extent much of this *Veda* is a repetition of the *Rig-Veda* sung in melodious format. Invocations of this *Veda* are primarily addressed to Soma (the Moon-god as well as the Soma drink), Agni (the fire god), and Indra (god of heaven). The *Chandogya Upanishad* came out of this *Veda*.

The *Atharva-Veda* is said to be the knowledge given by the Sage Atharvana. It has around 6000 verses. Some state that sage Atharvana did not formulate this *Veda* but was merely the chief priest in the ceremonies associated with it. Atharvana who is mentioned in the *Rig-Veda* was considered as the eldest son of Lord Brahma (God of creation). The *Atharva-Veda* is also known as *Brahma-Veda* because it is still used as a manual by Hindu priests and Brahmins. Ayurveda is a part of *Atharva-Veda*. A large number of *Upanishads* also came from the *Atharva-Veda*.

Brahmanas are other Vedic books that provide descriptions as well as directions for the performance of rituals. The word originated from the Brahmana priests who conduct the Vedic rituals.

Aryanyakas are additional books that contain mantras and interpretations of the Vedic rituals. These books also known as "forest books" since they were used by saints who had retired to meditate in the forests.

The *Upa-Vedas* are considered the smaller *Vedas*. They provide various sorts of knowledge and Vedic sciences. These include: 1. *Ayurveda*—Vedic science of health and longevity; 2. *Dharnur-Veda*—science of archery and war; 3. *Gandharva-Veda*—science of Music and Dance; 4. *Artha Shastra*—science of economics and government.

The *Vedangas* are also a group of scriptures attached to *Vedas* which also contain various Vedic sciences. These include:

1. Dharma Sutras—*Manu-samhita* or the law Codes of Manu, etc.
2. Jyotisha—Astrology and Astronomy
3. Kalpa—Rituals and legal matters
4. Siksha—Phonetics
5. Chhandas—Measurements
6. Nirukta—Etymology
7. Vyakarana—Sanskrit grammar

To explain a little further, Ayurveda is the Vedic scripture of medicine. It consisted of more than 100,000 verses initially. Still it is considered as an *Upa-Veda* of the *Atharva-Veda*. Sometimes this medical system is called part of the Fifth *Veda*. The Sanskrit word *Ayurveda* means medicine. The remedies in Ayurveda are mostly herbs and natural substances. The gods of healing in Ayurveda are Prajapati, Brihaspati, Indra, etc. Ayurveda originally classified diseases into physical, supernatural and spiritual. Ayurveda is practised widely in the State of Kerala in India. It is taught in the Ayurveda College, Kottakkal, Kerala.

The science of Jyotisha is meant as both astrology and astronomy. Both were part of the group known as the *Vedangas*. Astrology has come out of the Vedic sciences, and it does play a major part in the lives of people. It is still used widely for many purposes. The God of Astrology is Lord Subramaniyam, son of Lord Shiva. Some say that, once upon a time, astrology was a very well developed science, but today's astrology is only a skeleton of what it once was, with most of the valuable knowledge lost due to the practice of utmost secrecy by the learned men in Vedic society.

The *Upanishads* are texts by different saints that reveal ultimate truths. Many of them are connected with certain *Vedas*. The *Upanishads* basically explain the non-material aspect of the Absolute Truth and the oneness of Brahman. In this way, they do not really show that much about the personal nature of the Supreme Being. Thus, a person will not have much insight into the Supreme Being's personal form by studying only the *Upanishads*. However, some of them do go into introducing the fact that there is more to understand about God beyond the Brahman.

The *Upanishads* also help explain the spiritual dimension of our real identity and our qualities which are the same as the Brahman, but are different in quantity. We are the infinitesimal whereas the Brahman and Bhagavan are the Infinite. Yet, if one does not complete the study of the Vedic literature, a misinterpretation of the *Upanishads* may lead one to think that this oneness of spiritual quality between ourselves as the *jiva* souls and the Brahman means that we are the same as Brahman, or that we are the same as God. But that is not accurate.

There are a total of 108 major *Upanishads*, and many more minor ones. The are 13 principal *Upanishads* which are named after the sages. These are: 1. *Isa Upanishad*, 2. *Kena Upanishad*, 3. *Katha Upanishad*, 4. *Prasna Upanishad*, 5. *Mundaka Upanishad*, 6. *Mandukya Upanishad*, 7. *Aitareya Upanishad*, 8. *Taittiriya Upanishad*, 9. *Chandogya Upanishad*, 10. *Brihadaranyaka Upanishad*, 11. *Kaushitaki Upanishad*, 12. *Shvetashvatara Upanishad*, and 13. *Maitri Upanishad*.

The *Vedanta Sutras* are another important book that also goes on to explain spiritual truths to the aspirant. But these are presented in codes, or *sutras*, that were meant to be explained by the spiritual master. So any edition of the *Vedanta Sutras* will mostly have large purports that help explain the meaning of the *sutras*.

The basis of these explanations will depend on which school of thought in which the teacher has been trained. Thus, some will be more devotionally oriented, while others may be more inclined toward meditation on the impersonal Brahman. *Vedanta* essentially means the "End of the *Vedas*", or the end of all knowledge.

The *Itihasas* are the Vedic histories of the universe, known as the *Puranas*, which are a large and major portion of Vedic literature. The *Itihasas* also include the Vedic Epics, such as the *Ramayana* and the *Mahabharata*.

The *Ramayana* is the story of Lord Ramachandra, an incarnation of Lord Vishnu, and His princess Sita. It was written by Valmiki who wrote the whole *Ramayana* as the narration of a crying dove (who just lost her lover to a hunter's wicked arrow). The original text was written in very stylish Sanskrit language. This beautiful poem consists of 24,000 couplets. The *Ramayana* is a story which projects the Vedic ideals of life. There are many versions of the *Ramayana*. The Hindi version was written by sage Tulasi Das. The Malayalam version (Kerala state) was written by Thuncheth Ezuthachan.

The story in brief is as follows: Jealousy of his step-mother exiled Rama into the jungles along with his wife Sita and brother Lakshmana. There poor Sita was kidnapped by Ravana, the demon-king of Sri Lanka. Rama went to rescue her with the aid of the monkey-king Sugriva. In a great battle, Rama annihilated Ravana and his army. Thereafter, Rama along with Sita and Lakshmana returned triumphantly to their kingdom. Rama is an example of the perfect husband, Sita is the perfect wife, and Lakshmana is the perfect brother.

The *Ramayana* is a very cherished poem of the Hindus. The holy Deepavali festival is a celebration of victory of Rama over Ravana. Diwali or Deepavali is the "festival of lights" and is celebrated throughout India, when people put lit candles in their windows, or decorate their houses with lights, thus showing Rama the way home.

The *Mahabharata* is another of the world's great epics which consists of episodes, stories, dialogues, discourses and sermons. It contains 110,000 couplets or 220,000 lines in 18 *Parvas* or sections. It is the longest poem in the world. It is longer than Homer's Odyssey. It is the story of the Pandavas and Kauravas. The *Bhagavad-gita* is a chapter of the *Mahabharata*.

Apart from the 18 *Parvas* there is a section of poems in the form of an appendix with 16,375 verses which is known as *Harivamsa Parva*. So in total there are 19 *Parvas*, even though many saints do not consider the last *Parva* important.

The *Bhagavad-gita*, which means the song of Bhagavan, or God, is a part of the *Mahabharata*, appearing in the middle of it. Many consider the *Bhagavad-gita* as the most important of the Vedic scriptures and the essence of the *Upanishads* and Vedic knowledge. Anyone interested in the most important of the Eastern philosophy should read the *Bhagavad-gita*. If all the *Upanishads* can be considered as cows, then the *Bhagavad-gita* can be considered as milk.

The *Bhagavad-gita* consists of 18 chapters and over 700 verses. It deals with all types of yogas for the means of Self-realization. It is in the form of a very lively conversation between the warrior-prince Arjuna and his friend and charioteer Lord Krishna. This was spoken at the outset of the great *Mahabharata* war, in the middle of the battle field at Kuruksetra. This can still be visited just three hours north of New Delhi. Just before the beginning of the war, Arjuna refused to fight when he found he had to kill thousands of his own kinsmen to be victorious in the war. Lord Krishna advised him on a very large variety of subjects in a question and answer format. At the end, Arjuna took Lord Krishna's advice and fought and won a very fierce war. The *Gita* has an answer to every problem a man may face in his life. It never commands anyone what to do. Instead it discusses pros and cons of every action and thought. Throughout the *Gita* you will not come across any line starting or ending with Thou Shalt Not. That is the reason why the *Gita* is the darling of millions of seekers of truth throughout the world.

There are many versions of *Bhagavad-gita*. The very first English translation of the *Gita* was done by Charles Wilkins in 1785, with an introduction by Warren Hastings, the British Governor General of India. One of the most popular translations was done by Sir Edwin Arnold, under the title *The Song Celestial*. One of the most descriptive and accurate translations of the *Gita* was done by His Grace A. C. Bhaktivedanta Swami Prabhupada of the International Society for Krishna Consciousness, called *The Bhagavad-gita As It Is*. Almost all saints in India have published their versions of the *Bhagavad-gita*, some of which arrive at various conclusions or viewpoints in the commentary. So one does need to display some caution in picking which edition to read. Most intellectuals in the world go through the *Gita* at least once in their lifetime. Aldous Huxley wrote in his introduction of *The Song of God* by Swami Prabhavananda and Christopher Isherwood: "*The Bhagavad-gita* is perhaps the most systematic scriptural statement of the perennial philosophy". *The Gita* won the interest and admiration of great intellectuals such as Von Humboldt of Germany and Emerson of America. It has also influenced many Western thinkers, such as Hagel and Schopenhauer.

Robert Oppenheimer, the very first Chairman of Atomic Energy Commission and father of the Atom bomb was a great admirer of the *Bhagavad-gita*. He learnt

Sanskrit during the Manhattan Project to understand the true meaning of the *Gita*. He shocked the world when he quoted a couplet from the *Gita* (Chapter 11:12) after witnessing the first atomic explosion in the state of New Mexico, which reads, "If hundreds of thousands of suns rose up into the sky, they might resemble the effulgence of the Supreme Person in the universal form." Later when he addressed congress regarding the Atom Bomb he said the Atom Bomb reminded him of Lord Krishna who said in the *Bhagavad-gita*, "Time I am, the devourer of all."

The *Puranas* are the Vedic religious histories of the universe which expound various levels of the Vedic truths and provide deep elaborations of the knowledge presented in the earlier *Vedas*. They are divided into three sections. The six *Puranas* that are connected with Lord Vishnu are: 1. *Vishnu Purana*, 2. *Narada Purana*, 3. *Srimad Bhagavata Purana*, 4. *Garuda Purana*, 5. *Padma Purana*, and 6. *Varaha Purana*.

The six *Puranas* that are connected with Lord Siva are: 1. *Matsya Purana*, 2. *Kurma Purana*, 3. *Linga Purana*, 4. *Vayu Purana*, 5. *Skanda Purana*, and 6. *Agni Purana*.

The six *Puranas* that primarily are connected with Lord Brahma are: 1. *Brahma Purana*, 2. *Brahmanda Purana*, 3. *Brahma-Vaivasvata Purana*, or the *Brahma-Vaivarta Purana*, 4. *Markandeya Purana*, 5. *Bhavishya Purana*, and 6. *Vamana Purana*. Besides these, there are an additional 18 to 22 minor *Puranas*.

The 20 major *Puranas* include all the above as well as the *Shiva Purana* and the *Harivamsa Purana*. Of all *Puranas*, the *Srimad Bhagavata Purana*, which discusses the detailed pastimes of Lord Krishna, is considered one of the most important parts of the Vedic library. It contains 15,000 stanzas in 12 cantos. It was written by Sage Badarayana, also known as VedaVyasa or Vyasadeva. Vyasadeva, after writing all of His previous Vedic books, said the *Bhagavatam* was His own commentary and conclusion of all Vedic thought. The greatest exponent of the *Srimad-Bhagavatam* is Sage Suka, the son of Sage VedaVyasa. This book was recited to King Pariksit by Sage Suka in one week before the death of the King by the bite of a serpent. Much of the book is in dialogue form between King Pariksit and Sage Suka.

The *Srimad-Bhagavata* consists of stories of all the *avataras* of Lord Vishnu. The 10th chapter of the book deals with the story of Lord Krishna in detail. The last chapter deals exclusively with the Kali-Yuga, the present age, and about the last *avatara* of Lord Vishnu, Kalki. There is also a vivid description of the *Pralaya* or the great deluge in the last chapter.

According to the *Bhagavata Purana* the universe and creation came into existence because God in a pastime (*Lila*) willed to do so, and to manifest His inferior material energy. According to this scripture, there are nine different ways of exhibiting Bhakti or devotion to God like listening to stories of God, meditating, serving and adoring his image and finally self-surrender. This book is an authority on Vaishnavism and is a primary text for all Vaishnavas (worshipers of Lord Vishnu and His *avataras*) including those of the Hare Krishna Movement.

The *Agamas* are another group of scriptures that worship God in particular forms, and describe detailed courses of discipline for the devotee. Like the *Upanishads*, there are many *Agamas*. They can be broadly divided into three sets of *Agamas*, namely:
Vaishnava *Agamas*–the worship of Lord Vishnu;
Shaiva *Agamas*–the worship of Lord Shiva;
Shakti *Agamas*–the worship of the Mother Goddess.
There are no *Agamas* for Lord Brahma (God of creation). Shaivites have 28 *Agamas* and 108 *Upa Agamas* (minor *Agamas*). Shaktas recognize 77 *Agamas*. There are many Vaishnava *Agamas* of which the *Pancharatra* is one of the most important. Each *Agama* consists of philosophy, mental discipline, rules for constructing temples and religious practices.

The *Tantras* were started during the Vedic age and consist of cosmology, yogic exercises, etc. Tantra is very important and vast. The Sanskrit word *tantra* means to expand. Tantrism researched into Astronomy, Astrology, Palmistry, Cosmology, as well as the knowledge of the Chakras and Kundalini power, etc.

PRINCIPLE 24 & 25

The Vedic path consists of ten general rules of moral conduct. There are five for inner purity, called the *yamas*—*satya* or truthfulness, *ahimsa* or non-injury to others and treating all beings with respect, *asteya* or no cheating or stealing, *brahmacharya* or celibacy, and no selfish accumulation of resources for one's own purpose. The five rules of conduct for external purification are the *niyamas*—*shaucha* or cleanliness, *tapas* or austerity and perseverance, *aparighara* or purity of mind and body, *swadhyaya* or study of the *Vedas*, and *santosh* or contentment, and *ishwara-pranidhana*, acceptance of the Supreme.

There are also ten qualities that are the basis of *dharmic* (righteous) life. These are *dhriti* (firmness or fortitude), *kshama* (forgiveness), *dama* (self-control), *asteya* (refraining from stealing or dishonesty), *shauch* (purity), *indriya nigraha* (control over the senses), *dhih* (intellect), *vidya* (knowledge), *satyam* (truth) and *akrodhah* (absence of anger).

These are the most basic principles and moral rules of the Vedic tradition of behavior, before getting into more specific instructions that deal with higher principles of Self-realization. However, any religious process should include these basic Dharmic rules if it is to be considered effective at all. Without these basic regulations, it can hardly be regarded as an uplifting process for advancing one's consciousness. If a person does not know or cannot follow the basics such as these, there can be little expectation for one's spiritual development. That is why the Vedic tradition outlines these elementary principles and every Dharmist knows this standard.

5

Sanatana-Dharma: Its Real Meaning

When it comes to understanding the full meaning of Sanatana-dharma, we have to be aware of its Sanskrit definition. The root of the word *dharma* comes from *dhri*, which means to uphold or maintain. The Sanskrit says *dharayati iti dharmaha*, which translates as dharma is that which upholds. However, not only what is supported is dharma, but that which does the supporting is also dharma, *dhriyate iti dharmaha*. So dharma consists of both the force that sustains as well as what is sustained. It can also be said that there is the path of dharma as well as its conclusion, the object of dharma, or what we are seeking, the goal of life. So dharma is the means as well as the goal.

Dharma is also said to be the force which maintains the universe. Where there is dharma there is harmony and balance, both individually, socially and inter-galactically. So the path of dharma brings about the harmony and contentment that is also another aspect of what we are seeking. In this way, we want harmony inwardly, in our own consciousness, but we also cannot have individual peace unless there is harmony or cooperation socially, amongst the masses. So where there is no dharma, there is disharmony and a state of being that is out of balance. And socially it means that without dharma, there is a lack of cooperation, along with escalating quarrel and fighting. This often manifests as a lack of distribution of resources, whereas some parts of the world may experience abundance of water, food or fuel, yet other parts are starving. Or by dishonest manipulation of supply and demand some necessities become priced so high that they are out of reach for the poor. When we act against the law of dharma, we disrupt the very harmony and cooperation that we want. In other words, we create a life for our-selves in which there is stress, confusion, discontent, and frustration. And when we feel that way, that becomes our contribution to the general social condition. It is the exact opposite of what we wish to attain. Thus, to live a life outside of dharma means to work against ourselves.

Furthermore, if we live on the basis of lust and greed, to accumulate possessions, money, and sensual pleasure by the demands of the mind and senses, it will become most difficult to follow the path of dharma. Of course, when this is the case, we often see that such people become increasingly discontent and out of balance, enamored by the illusory happiness in material existence. Doing what should not be done is called *vidharma*, which is a type of *adharma* or nondharmic activity. The conclusion, therefore, is that if we want happiness and peace we must learn how to live according to the path of dharma.

The practice of dharma should be done not out of compulsion but out of love due to the perception of the Supreme in all living beings. With this motivation, dharma can assist in preventing injury to others and treating each other respectfully. Dharma also means righteous conduct. This includes following social laws and proper moral activity and behavior. It encourages truthfulness of thought, word and deed. The point of which is to reach the goal of dharma.

Dharma also means truth. So we follow the path of dharma to free ourselves from illusion and reach the ultimate Truth, which is the topmost reality, the spiritual strata. The Absolute Truth means the final philosophical goal and end of all knowledge, Vedanta, which is God, the Supreme Being. So when we want to attain liberation from material existence, after realizing the futility of its temporary nature, and wish to reach God, then it becomes much easier to follow the path of dharma and overcome the temptations of the temporary material world. Then we can let go of the illusory objects that are, in fact, hurdles on the path to Truth and God.

The more we are attracted to the material existence and in accumulating the illusory objects to satisfy our mind and senses, in essence, the more hurdles we bring into our life. And we must overcome these obstructions at some point to reach the Absolute Truth. Therefore, life lived according to the law of dharma means the freer we become from false obstacles, from stress, from false hangups and mood swings, and inner conflicts. Thus, the freer we are to experience our real selves as spiritual beings. And the more society chooses to follow the path of dharma, the more easily we can attain an existence of cooperation and harmony instead of one of wars, conflict, terror and killing. So whatever we do, even if it is doing business, making money, politics, etc., it should be done on the basis of dharma. Then things will progress in the proper way. Following dharma will bring both material well-being as well as final liberation. Thus, one can attain all that this world can offer through the path of dharma.

On a national, ethnic, or racial level, dharma is an instrument of unity, not divisiveness. That which helps unite everyone and develop love and universal brotherhood is dharma. That which causes discord or disharmony or provokes hatred is *adharma*. With this understanding we can perceive that certain religions that exist on this planet that encourage divisiveness between those that are "saved" and those that are supposedly going to hell, or which primarily focus on differences between their sect and others, are actually *adharmic*. Those religions that do not teach that we are all children of the same God, all equal in the eyes of God, are *adharmic*. They may merely be limited in their depth of knowledge and awareness, but until they adopt the dharmic principles they will continue to produce disagreements, restlessness, harsh attitudes and even hatred amongst people in the name of religion. The reason is that they are absent of real transcendental knowledge and deep spiritual insights. Since they lack dharma, they will not be able to deliver one to dharma. Thus, lack of peace and harmony amongst various religions will be commonplace until this is remedied. In this way, the path of dharma is more than a religion or belief system. It is the means to directly perceive and live according to that higher reality and unity between us all.

So we can see that the path of dharma is more of a way of life. Some people may say that Vedic dharma, or Hinduism, is another religion. Yet, if we understand this principle of dharma, we can see that it is not merely another religion or "ism". It is a way of life that is lived with every moment and every breath. It is a matter of raising our consciousness to the highest level possible. Thus, we reach our fullest potential, which in the end is on the spiritual platform and the perception of the spiritual dimension.

For example, when one comes to the level of dharma, then all of his or her actions are in accordance with the dharma, the path of harmony and balance, in tune with the Divine. In Vedic culture we can find the artful expression of dance. This is just one of many art forms in the Vedic tradition. But on the path of dharma it is an expression of one's emotional outlet toward God, Ishwara or Krishna. An emotional outlet in this manner means you express yourself to God, you release your love for God and your thoughts and consciousness become more absorbed in God. So this is also like yoga, a form of dedicated meditation. In this way, the attitude within the dance is unique. It is not merely an emotional release for satisfying one's own mind, but it is an expression of longing toward becoming united with God. That is yoga. It is dharma. So in this sense, dharma means the freedom to naturally express our inner proclivity, which is to get closer to the Absolute Truth, and worship this Truth, this Ishvara or God.

Therefore, on the path of dharma, the dances, the movements, the costumes and jewelry, are all used to either relate the pastimes of God or to enhance our attachment to God. So these are all expressions of dharma, our eternal nature to love God and be loved by God. Thus, dharma is also protected by continuing the tradition. For this reason there needs to be a class of men who are dedicated to protect the dharma. It is only one who has the dharma that can protect it.

Now when we add the word Sanatana to dharma, it expands the meaning and purpose. Sanatana means eternal. So Sanatana-dharma can mean the ancient path that has existed from time immemorial. It is the eternal path which has been given to humanity and comes from beyond the material dimension. Sanatana-dharma is the inter-dimensional path of progress for all living beings.

It can also be said to be the unceasing and imperishable path of the soul. Sanatana-dharma also means the eternal path and our eternal nature. Dharma means the ultimate nature of the living being, the spirit soul. And the nature or dharma of the soul is to love and be loved, to serve its most lovable object and to receive love. Just like the dharma or nature of sugar is to be sweet, we know that if it is not sweet or if it is salty, then it is not sugar. The dharma of fire is to give light and heat. If it does not do that, then it cannot be fire. So the Sanatana-dharma or eternal nature of the soul is that it is a spiritual being that is naturally connected to God and feels the greatest joy in its constitutional position as a servant of God. The soul needs to love. It cannot do without it. And our nature as human beings reflects the nature of the soul because we are always looking for love. Although when such love is interpreted through the mind and senses, it is often accepted as the satisfaction of the mind and body. This only brings temporary happiness because it is merely a reflection of what we really want and need. So for the soul, the most lovable object is the Lord and the most pleasing things are spiritual relations and exchanges. This is what will give the epitome of bliss that we long for in loving relationships.

So Sanatana-dharma means both the ultimate spiritual truth and the means to attain it. And that truth is the divine knowledge of the soul. So if there is to be any eternality in our relationships, or any spiritual connection with anything we do, it has to be based on that divine knowledge of the soul, the ultimate reality. That is the path of Sanatana-dharma, to realize our spiritual identity and then know how to act accordingly.

Therefore, the purpose of life is to follow the path of dharma which will bring us to the conclusion of recognizing that everything is the energy of God, brahman. Following this further, the path of dharma will bring us into union with God. And the highest union is through love and devotion, or *bhakti*. Thus bhakti-yoga, the process of loving devotion to the Lord, is the epitome of following Sanatana-dharma. Making this the goal of our life means that we are living a life of dharma. And the ultimate goal of dharma is to reach God.

Sanatana-dharma is also a matter of understanding. It is an awareness that every particle of this universe is an expansion of God's energies. That it is all an exhibition of the potencies of the Para-Brahman, the Absolute Existence. Dharma is the path to seeing how God is everywhere. Thus, dharma is not only the path to God but is also in God. A truly liberated person does not worry about liberation, or in going home back to God in the spiritual world. He is already aware that he is in God's energy, whether it is the material or spiritual energy. For him, everything is an exhibition of God's potencies wherever he goes. Thus, the *dharmin* (also called a Dharmist or Dharmi), the follower of dharma who sees God everywhere, is already home. Liberation from material existence will follow such a person like a servant.

If we understand this properly, we can see that Sanatana-dharma is the basis of universal truth. It can be applied to anyone at anytime and anywhere in the universe. Thus, many religions can and should include Sanatana-dharma within their approach and outlook in order to be complete. It does not matter in which religion you may be affiliated, you can still benefit and grow within the fold of Sanatana-dharma to reach a higher awareness and perception of your true potential and genuine spiritual identity. In this way, the whole world could reach a new stage in its social and spiritual development, as well as in harmony and cooperation.

6

The Power of the Dharma

The Power of the Dharma is found in the number of tools it has always provided in order for humanity to reach its fullest potentials, both as individuals who are searching for their own fulfillment and spiritual awakening, and as a society that can function in harmony with nature and cooperation amongst themselves.

By investigating the knowledge and viewpoints in the many topics found in Vedic culture, we can certainly see that the practice and utilization of this Vedic knowledge can indeed assist us in many ways. And in regard to all the trouble we presently find in this world, maybe it is time to look at things through a different and deeper view to find the answers and directions that are so needed. The knowledge and understandings of this great Vedic culture may indeed be what will help us see through the fog of confusion that seems to envelope so much of the world.

What we find in Vedic culture are areas of study, progress and expression that are as relevant today for human advancement as they were hundreds or thousands of years ago. India and its Vedic culture has contributed much to the world, such as its music, beautiful forms of art and architecture, martial arts, astronomy, holistic medicine in Ayurveda, and the mathematical system based on the number ten, along with its yoga and philosophy. In the United States, yoga has exploded into a three billion dollar industry. A recent survey (at the time of this writing in 2005) showed that 16.5 million people are practicing yoga, or 7.5 percent of the United States. Also, the Yoga Journal magazine has grown from a circulation of 90,000 in 1998, to 170,000 in 2000, to 325,000 in 2005.

Another example is Vedic mathematics which is an ancient development that continues to play an important part in modern society. Without the advancements in math that had been established by Vedic culture as far back as 2500 BC and passed along to others, such as the Greeks and Romans, we would not have many of the developments and inventions that we enjoy today. The Greek alphabet, for instance, was a great hindrance to calculating. The Egyptians also did not have a numerical system suitable for large calculations. For the number 986 they had to use 23 symbols. Even after the Greeks, the Romans also were in want of a system of mathematical calculations. Only after they adopted the Indian system that was called Arabic numerals did they find what they needed. Weights and measures and scales with decimal divisions had been found from that period and were still quite accurate.

The difference was that Vedic mathematics had developed the system of tens, hundreds, thousands, etc., and the basis of carrying the remainder of one column of numbers over to the next. This made for easy calculations of large numbers that was nearly impossible in other systems, as found with the Greeks, Romans, Egyptians and even Chinese. The Vedic system had also invented the zero, which has been called one of the greatest developments in the history of mathematics.

The numeral script from India is said to have evolved from the Brahmi numerals. This spread to Arabia through traders and merchants, and from there up into Europe and elsewhere. It became known as the Arabic numerals, yet the Arabians had called them "Indian figures" (*Al-Arqan-Al-Hindu*) and the system of math was known as *hindisat*, or the Indian art.

Vedic culture already had an established mathematical system that had been recorded in the *Shulba Sutras*. These are known to date back to the 8th century BC. The name *Shulba Sutras* meant "codes of rope". This was because such calculations were used for measuring precise distances for altars and temple structures by using lengths of rope.

The *Shulba Sutras* were actually a portion of a larger text on mathematics known as the *Kalpa Sutras*. These and the Vedic mathematicians were recognized for their developments in arithmetic and algebra. Indians were the first to use letters of the alphabet to represent unknowns. But they were especially known for what they could do in geometry. In fact, geometrical instruments had been found in the Indus Valley dating back to 2500 BC. Furthermore, what became known as the Pythagorean theorem was already existing in the *Baudhayana*, the earliest of the *Shulba Sutras* before the 8th century BC. This was presented by Pythagoras around 540 BC after he discovered it in his travels to India or his contacts with traveling merchants or Brahmins who had come from India. So this shows the advanced nature of the Vedic civilization.

After the *Shulba Sutras*, Vedic mathematics enjoyed further development in the field of Jyotish, Vedic astronomy, which used all forms of math. Indian mathematicians continued creating systems that were not known in Europe until much later in the Renaissance period. For example, Aryabhatta in the 5th century introduced sines and versed sines, and is credited as the inventor of algebra. He is said to be the first to state that the Earth travels around the sun. However, the ancient Vedic texts have described this many years earlier, which shows the wisdom of the early Vedic seers.

Aryabhatta was followed by Brahmagupta (7th century) who was the great mathematician that especially developed the use of zero and was the first to use algebra to solve problems in astronomy. Next was Mahavira (9th century) who made great strides in the use of fractions and figuring out how to divide one fraction by another. Then there was Bhaskara (12th century) who made progress in spherical trigonometry and principles of calculus before Newton by 500 years. He used it to determine the daily motion of planets.

The Vedic system of math, as explained in the *sutras*, also reduced the number of steps in calculations to merely a few that otherwise required many steps by conventional methods. Thus, this ancient science is still worthy of study today.

A well-developed medical system was also in existence by the 1st century A.D. Progress in medicine led to developments in chemistry and the production of medicine, alkaline substances and glass. Colorfast dies and paints were developed to remain in good condition over the centuries. The paintings in the caves of Ajanta are a testimony to this.

Vedic art is another ancient development that still holds much appreciation in modern times. Art in the Vedic tradition was never a mere representation of an artist's imagination. It was always a vehicle to convey higher truths and principles, levels of reality that may exist beyond our sense perception. It was always used to bring us to a higher purpose of existence and awareness. In this way, it was always sacred and beheld the sacred. Still today it is used to allow others to enter into a transcendental experience. It may also present the devotional objects of our meditation.

Vedic paintings or symbols are unique in that they can deliver the same spiritual energy, vibration and insight that it represents. In other words, through the meditation and devotional mood of the artist, the art becomes a manifestation of the higher reality. In this way, the painting or symbol becomes the doorway to the spiritual essence contained within. They are like windows into the spiritual world. Through that window we can have the experience of what is called *darshan* of the Divine or divinities, God or His associates. Darshan is not merely seeing the Divine but it is also entering into the exchange of seeing and being seen by the Divine.

Thus the art, or the deity, is beyond mundane principles or ingredients, such as paint, paper, stone or metal with which it may be made, but it becomes completely spiritual through which the deity can reveal Himself or Herself. Thus, the truth of spiritual reality can pierce through the darkness of the material energy and enter our mind and illuminate our consciousness.

To convey higher realities in paintings and sculpture, everything has a meaning. The postures, gestures, colors, instruments or weapons, everything conveys a principle or purpose, which often must be explained to those who lack understanding. Thus, knowing the inner meaning of the painting increases its depth for those who can perceive it, which makes it worthy of further meditation and contemplation.

As with art, dance in India was not merely an expression of an artist's emotional mindset or imagination, but was meant to be an interpretation or conveyance of higher spiritual principles or pastimes of the Divine. In fact, in the Vedic pantheon Shiva is known as Nataraja, the king of dancers. Shiva's dance was also not without a more significant purpose. His dance was based on the rhythm of cosmic energy that pervades the universe, and the destruction of the illusory energy by which all souls are given the opportunity for release from the illusion to attain liberation, *moksha*.

In this way, traditional Indian dance is highly spiritual and often accompanies important religious rituals and holy days and festivals. Vedic dance goes back to prehistoric times. Bharata Muni wrote his *Natya Shastra*, science of drama and dance, over 2000 years ago. In it he explains that it was Lord Brahma, the secondary engineer of the universal creation, who brought dance (*natya*) and drama to the people of Earth millions of years ago, shortly after the Earth was created.

Now dance has evolved into a tradition involving various schools and styles but with strict discipline. It is not uncommon that Indian families will have their daughters spend at least several years or more in such study and practice. There is a precise method of postures, facial and hand gestures (*mudras*), and movements, along with footwork that must be learned and synchronized to the beat and music in order to convey specific meanings, moods and stories to the audience. Many temples, especially in South India, were known for maintaining large groups of dancers that performed at festivals and religious functions.

When the dance is performed according to the spiritual standards, which some view as similar to the practice of yoga, even the dancers can invoke a high degree of spirituality in their own consciousness and bring unity between their inner selves and God. Then the transcendental atmosphere can manifest and draw the Divine to appear in the performers on stage. Thus, the environment becomes transformed and the audience may also experience *darshan* of the Divine and experience an inspiring upliftment in their own consciousness. In this way, the dance is divine beauty in motion. Or it is a way of invoking the spiritual dimension into our midst. Few other forms of dance attempt to do this.

Various schools of dance include Bharata Natyam, Kathakali, Manipuri, Orissi, Kathak, Mohini Atam, Krishna Atam, Bhagavata Mela, etc. Thus, we may have many dances that convey stories from the *Ramayana* and *Mahabharata*, or Krishna-lila from the *Bhagavata Purana*. Nowadays this ancient art of Indian dance is enjoying a wide audience and a prominent place on the international stage.

So, as we can see, Vedic culture and its many areas of knowledge and devotional expression are still as relevant today as it was thousands of years ago. And humanity can benefit from it from introspection and spiritual as well as material development as it did in the past.

AYURVEDA

Ayurveda is the Vedic system of holistic medicine. It has become quite popular in the West and is continuing to gain ground and acceptance. To understand briefly what Ayurveda is, I let Pratichi Mathur, an Ayurvedic practitioner herself, tell us about it from the book, "Vedic Culture: The Difference It Can Make in Your Life":

"So what is Ayurveda exactly? Literally translated from Sanskrit it is composed of two words '*Ayus*' which means life and '*Veda*' which denotes knowledge. So Ayurveda is the knowledge of healthy living and is confined not only to the treatment of diseases. Life is a vast, and an all-encompassing phenomena, which includes death. On one end, life is a celebration of birth, growth, child bearing, youth and sexuality; on the other end, life also brings forth disease, decay, aging, and loss of vigor. Ayurveda is that ancient art and science that helps us understand this very 'life' with all its different shades and colors; understand how best we can undertake this journey; and how we transition through its different phases, example from teenage, to adulthood, to maturity, etc. Following the principles of Ayurveda brings about a profound understanding of the inner ability to have sound body, mind and spirit. From this point of view, Ayurveda is a compendium of life and not disease. This is a major agenda indeed for any system of medicine, but can it be any less—especially if true healing has to take place. Perhaps, this is exactly why Ayurveda manages to get to the root of the disease that distresses the mind or the emotion that ails the body.

"Ayurveda has twin objectives—maintaining the health of the healthy, and cure illnesses of the diseased. Ayurveda, which is not just a system of disease and its management, but literally a living dynamic philosophy and manual on the art of living, is well fitted to meet its objectives. On one hand Ayurveda offers treatments like *Panchakarma* or even surgery for the diseased; and on the other hand Ayurveda offers preventative medicine for the healthy. These include elaborate details for following ideal daily and seasonal routines, specialized diets for optimizing health and immunity (Ojas), *Rasayana Chikitsa* (promotive therapy), *Vajikarna Chikitsa* (aphrodisiac therapy), *Swasthavritta* (regimen to stay healthy furnishing details on topics such as exercise, smoking for health), *Sadachar* (social hygiene), etc.

"Ayurveda advocates a complete promotive, preventive and curative system of medicine and includes eight major clinical specialties of medicine namely, (1) Medicine (*Kayachikitsa*), (2) Surgery (*Salya Tantra*), (3) ENT (*Salakya Tantra*), (4) Pediatrics (*Kaumatabhritya*), (5) Psychiatry (*Bhutvidya*), (6) Toxicology (*Agad Tantra*), (7) Nutrition, rejuvenation and geriatrics (*Rasayan tantra*), and (8) Sexology and virilization (*Vajikarana*). This shows what a developed science Ayurveda was in ancient times.

"The exact origin of Ayurveda is lost in the mists of antiquity. Since Panini is placed at 7th century BC and Ayurveda depicts non-Paninian Sanskrit grammar, it is logical to place Ayurveda between 6th–10th Century BC. Tracing the continuity of Ayurveda, it is natural to look for the continuing thread in India's ancient Vedic tradition. Although the term Ayurveda, does not seem to appear in the *Vedas*, and it appears first in Panini's *Ashtadhayayi*, however, there are positive evidences to show that in the Vedic period, medicine as a profession was prevalent. The *Rig Veda* and the *Atharva Veda* both mention that there were thousands of medical practitioners and thousands of medicines. References to Ayurveda are found as early as the *Rig Veda*. The three Rig Vedic gods Indra, Agni and Soma relate to the three biological humors: Vata, Pitta and Kapha. References are made of organ transplants as in the case of the artificial limb of queen Vishpala, daughter of King Khela. The functions of physicians are also described in the *Rig Veda*.

"Rishi Sushruta, famous Ayurvedic Surgeon, also holds that Ayurveda is a supplement (*upanga*) of the *Atharva Veda*. While several other sources including the famous Hindu epic *Mahabharata* speak of Ayurveda as an *upanga* of *Atharva Veda*; several other schools of thought hold Ayurveda as a fifth Veda (*Panchamveda*). Perhaps Ayurveda grew from *Atharva Veda* first as a branch and then as a comprehensive vast system deserving it's own satus, or it developed parallel to the four *Vedas* as an independent knowledge (with close resembalance to the *Atharva Veda*)."

JYOTISH

Jyotish is the Vedic form of astrology, which is an ancient science and is also being accepted and gaining popularity in the West. Vedic Astrology is meant to help the individual better find his or her way through life. It is to assist in discovering one's highest proclivities, personality, character, qualities and traits and what may be one's best direction for a career, and other things. Thus a person will least likely waste one's time in unfulfilling activities, professions or pursuits.

To further our understanding of Jyotish, I let Chakrapani Ullal, one of the most well-known Vedic Astrologers in the West, describe it as taken from the book, "Vedic Culture: The Difference It Can Make in Your Life":

"We turn our attention now to the subject of a branch of the *Vedas* called Vedic astrology or Jyotish, which is called the 'eye of the *Vedas*'. It has a cognizing influence of the truth of life and self-knowledge. It acts as a mirror to an individual without which one may not know how to approach life most effectively. It is also called the 'Science of Time'. Time is the source power that rules the universe. All things originate through the procession of time. Hence, Vedic Astrology constitutes the science that maps the structure of time. Astrology is considered divine knowledge that is pure, supreme, secret, and exalted.

"Astrology can be defined as the science of correlations of astronomical facts with terrestrial events, and demonstrates the Vedic understanding of the universal interconnectedness and interdependence of all phenomenon, that microcosm and macrocosm are but reflections of one another. Just as mathematics is the organizing principle of science when dealing with inanimate matter, so also astrology is the organizing principle which deals with life and its significance in relation to all living bodies. The planets are seen as reflectors or transmitters of light and solar energy. The solar and planetary rays, like radio waves, affect biological and psychological processes. The rays of influence are unseen vibrations that are not perceptible to the physical eye.

"Astrology gives insight and guidance to the fortunes and misfortunes of men, issues of empires and republics, floods and earthquakes, volcanic eruptions, plagues, pestilence and other incidents concerning terrestrial phenomena in relation to the regular movements of the planets.

"Over 10,000 years ago the ancient sages, in their super-conscious state, cognized that there is energy in planets, and that they send out different rays at different angles which bear influence on everything animate and inanimate on other planets. Through their sensitized intuition and repeated observations these highly evolved souls were able to find out the different characteristics inborn in the planets and also discovered that each rules a distinctive part of the human mind/body. It was also found that particular groups of stars known as constellations have different characteristics, and that they modulate the influence of the planets.

"Astrologers say that there are two forces, Daiva and Purushakara, fate and individual energy. The individual energy can modify and even frustrate fate. Moreover, the stars often indicate several fate possibilities; for example, that one may die in mid-age, but that if, through determination, one gives attention in that area it can be overcome, one can live to a predictable old age. Thus, astrology does not say that events must and should happen, but gives the benefic and malefic tendencies which can be directed or modified through conscious effort. The horoscope shows a man's character and temperament. Though it may show that he could become a criminal, it does not mean he is fated to become so. What it means is that he is just the sort of person who will have criminal tendencies, but they can be checked by proper care and training. Additionally, if emotional and financial challenges are indicated in any particular year, one can certainly meet the crisis better if one knows that it might occur.

"Then, how would one define astrology? It is the philosophy of discovering and analyzing past impulses and future actions of both individuals and nations in the light of planetary configurations. Astrology explains life's reactions to planetary vibrations."

VEDIC GEMOLOGY

Gemology is an important field in today's market. But when we speak of Vedic gemology, we do not mean that it is merely for judging the value of a gem. The Vedic purpose in gemology is to determine the best type of quality gem for a person to wear. Thus, Vedic gemology worked in conjunction with Ayurveda and Jyotish to establish the best gem a person should wear for health and positive influence. To give a little more understanding about this increasingly recognized field, I include the following description by Howard Beckman, a qualified and practicing Vedic gemologist, from the book, "Vedic Culture: The Difference It Can Make in Your Life":

"It is a field that is making great strides medically by using gems for illness and disease both of the physical body and the mind. It is a noninvasive therapy that has produced definite repeatable results medically. (It should be noted that only natural gems, not synthetic, have this inherent energy and also that certain gem treatments commonly used for color or clarity enhancement will render the gem 'dead' and ineffective.) Our research and record keeping of case histories of gem use in jewelry for astrological reasons has also allowed us to not only prove the efficacy of gems, but in "debunking" commonly held incorrect notions as far as how to recommend them, as well as baseless superstitions.

"It is the energy force of the cosmos that sustains all living organisms. This energy is called '*prana*'. It energizes our bodies throughout life until it leaves at the time of death, leaving the gross material body to decay and return to the elements from which it arose. The Vedic scriptures calculate our life spans in the number of breaths we are allotted during our lives. If we use this energy more quickly, then the life span will be shorter. (Long distance runners are renowned for dying in their 50's.) If we conserve our energy, especially through systems such as the yoga system, then the life span may be extended. The Ayurvedic system of healing first evaluates the intake and distribution of *prana* within both the physical and subtle (ethereal) bodies of an individual.

"Gem therapy has been used by many ancient cultures and especially the wearing of gemstones on the body had great significance for the Vedic culture, other than the purely cosmetic or ornamental value that gems are mostly used for today. The science of Ayurveda when combined with Vedic astrology gives a wealth of knowledge in the correct application of gemstones to amplify planetary rays, which can have a dynamic effect on one's physical and emotional health, one's ability to prosper materially, and the general well-being of individual persons here on earth.

"As gems have such vibratory qualities, we may utilize them to not only affect the brain, but also the higher vibrations in the physical body necessary for healthy functioning of all our internal and external organs. Dr. Young and Bruce Tainio of Cheny University in Washington have made the following statements from their research in this regard. 'The average frequency of the human body during the daytime is between 62 and 68 cycles per second. If it drops below this rate the immune defense system will start to shut down. Cold symptoms appear at 58 cycles, flu at 57, candida at 55, glandular fever at 52, and cancer at 42 cycles per second'.

"Natural (meaning from the earth, which does not include synthetic, manmade material), untreated gemstones, which are repositories of cosmic colors, can restore the *pranic* energy to the cells of the body, so that its natural vibratory rate and normal health may be regained when it is in a diseased condition. Blue sapphire can tranquilize or have a sedative effect. Emerald can be used as an analgesic. Yellow sapphire has antiseptic properties, and diamond's ability to stimulate cell growth are just a few examples of how gems can affect the healing process in the body."

VASTU SHASTRA

Vāstu is the Vedic science of architectural and home arrangement. It made its way through the orient and became known as Feng Shui, which has made particular progress in popularity in the West. However, Vāstu is a particular science that deals with the flow of energy through a house or building for the highest benefits. It is not enough to merely arrange a house so it looks nice or that there is a good flow of energy through it. But there is much that depends on the directions in which things are facing or which parts of the building in which certain activities are performed.

To get a little more insight into the Vedic science of Vāstu, I have included the following description by Arun Naik, an architect that practices the science and art of Vāstu Shāstra. Again, this is taken from the book, "Vedic Culture: The Difference It Can Make in Your Life":

"The Vedic and the Agamic traditions of ancient India always held that the microcosm is a reflection of the macrocosm. A dwelling is an ecological unit, a microcosm which reflects the Cosmos, the macrocosm. Vāstu Shāstra is the applied aspect of this philosophy, a highly refined method of creating a living space which is a miniature replica of the cosmos as perceived by the *Vedas*. Vāstu Shāstra is about emulating the attributes of the Cosmic Space, about bringing the divine sentinels of Cosmic Directions into our homes, about creating Harmony by creating a living environment where the forces of nature are balanced and at peace with each other.

"Sri Aurobindo has said…'Indian sacred architecture of whatever date, style or dedication goes back to something timelessly ancient and now outside India almost wholly lost, something which belongs to the past, and yet it goes forward too, though this the rationalistic mind will not easily admit, to something which will return upon us and is already beginning to return, something which belongs to the future.' (SA, *The Renaissance in India*)

"There is a prayer in *Sama Veda*:

May there be peace in the sky, may there be peace in mid region, may there be peace on earth, may there be peace in the waters, may the medicinal plants be peaceful, may the forest be peaceful, may there be peace in gods, may Brahma be peaceful, may all the creation be peaceful, may there be peace and peace only, may such peace come to us.

"Vāstu is about creating an Inner Space, the *chidakash*, where this divine peace can park itself. And it achieves it by creating a harmonious external environment—the *bahyakash*.

"At a more earthly level, Vāstu Shāstra aims at establishing a dynamic balance between Form and Energy so that harmonious conditions are created for the inhabitants. Vāstu buildings have harmonious energies and they promote stability, prosperity, happiness, and mental peace for the occupants and owners.

"The principle of Vāstu is that the Cosmic World with its order and stern discipline has been built by the gods who occupy all the spaces, from the celestial Space within the Cosmic World to the little spaces in our homes, and even our mental space, *chidambaram*. Man's existence in the Cosmic World has a purpose: it must ascend to immortality and godhood; and the gods, having occupied man's inner Space, strive to create different states in man's consciousness for his ascension from mortality and low nature to Truth, godhood and immortality. Vāstu Shāstra helps the effort of the gods by creating an external space—a dwelling, a place to worship and meditate, or a place to work by applying the same laws which the gods have used to create the Cosmic World. This, indeed, is the ultimate function and the highest objective of Vāstu Shāstra."

So here we can see how various aspects of the ancient Vedic culture are still applicable today and can provide assistance in our attempts to reach our highest potential, both materially and spiritually. This is the constant and higher nature of the power of the dharma.

7

The Vedic Spiritual Paths to Liberation

Besides the various Vedic sciences that tend towards the material benefits, the Vedic culture is well known for its philosophy and practices and traditions that can take a person deeply into the spiritual domain. The Vedic system does not teach that you can only connect with God through a church, an institution, or that it depends on the approval of a cleric or priest. The Vedic process gives you the tools and methods so that a person can purify and change one's own consciousness to be able to one day perceive the spiritual strata. Other religions may offer a doctrine to believe in, often proclaiming that accepting it is all you need and your search for spiritual truth need not continue or go beyond that because you have already reached the goal. But in actuality if you do not continue to improve, then you remain incomplete on the spiritual journey. Belief or faith is only the beginning. They are the keys for opening the door while the complete journey is on the other side.

The Vedic process is to assist everyone in developing their own God-realization. Thus, the Vedic system focuses on personal *sadhana* or spiritual practice to attain spiritual transformation. Of these, there are four basic paths that are recommended within the Vedic system. These include:

1. Jnana-yoga—Path of Knowledge

2. Karma-yoga—Path of Selfless Actions

3. Raja-yoga—Path of Breath Control and Pranayama

4. Bhakti-yoga—Path of Devotion to God

All of these methods can interact with and assist the others.

Jnana-yoga. This is the path to enlightenment through the process of mental speculation and the study and acquirement of empirical knowledge. On a deeper level, *jnana* (pronounced gyana) or jnana-yoga is the process of discriminating between truth and non-truth, or reality and *maya*, and understanding what is the Divine. This is the knowledge of the soul and God, and the relationship between them.

The aspirant of jnana-yoga engages in long hours of study and discussion in the attempt to understand the highest truth so the *jnana*, or knowledge, becomes *vijnana*, realized knowledge as opposed to merely acquired or studied knowledge. One following this path must also accept the authority of the great sages and study in their association. Without proper guidance along this path one can easily become confused about what is actually the Absolute Truth. Thus, one must rise above the mental platform or cognitive intellect and take up the practice wherein one's consciousness actually starts to change and progress, or purify to be able to perceive the spiritual dimension. Therefore, the acquirement of *jnana* or spiritual knowledge is one of the first steps in spiritual development. It is the start of the spiritual path, but it must then be followed by a practical *sadhana* in which one engages in direct spiritual practices. So from Jnana-yoga, a person often includes one of the other types of yoga.

Karma-yoga. The word *karma* is derived from the Sanskrit word *Kri* meaning "to do". The word *karma* is used in many areas of Vedic philosophy. Here the meaning of karma is work. When we breathe, it is karma. When we think, it is karma. The actions we do accumulate karma and dictate our past, present and future.

Karma is categorized by three forces. They are *Tamas, Rajas* and *Sattva*, which are the modes of material nature. *Tamas* represents inactivity and darkness. *Rajas* represents activity and passion. *Sattva* is the mode of goodness and light. Karma-yoga involves properly employing these three factors to raise the qualities of our activities.

Karma-yoga has a lot to do with Bhakti-yoga and Jnana-yoga. Chapters 3, 4, and 5 of the *Bhagavad-gita* explain Karma-yoga.

Karma-yoga in brief is about attaining freedom through unselfish actions, "Nishkama Karma". Selfish actions retard our goal. Unselfish actions take us towards our goal. So Karma-yoga is the system of attaining freedom from all karma through properly directed selfless actions.

Raja-yoga. This is a more scientific path of God-realization. In this path, God is more or less treated as Pure Energy. Sage Patanjali, the author of the *Yoga Sutras*, was the first to systematize the practices of this technical yoga. Patanjali defined yoga as *Chitta-Vritti-Nirodha*, which is explained as:

Yoga—union with the divine or salvation.

Chitta—mind.

Vritti—modifications or vibrations.

Nirodha—stoppage or suppression or restraint.

So according to Sage Patanjali, "The union with the Divine or salvation means stoppage of the vibrations or modifications of the mind." In Raja-yoga, a devotee uses meditation to try to achieve a state above the mind, free from all its dictates and interferences. It is very difficult to explain in simple terms, and thus it is rather difficult to use this system successfully in this age. The ordinary man whose consciousness is confined to the lower mind can conceive of only concrete images of objects, which are derived through the sense-organs. In a nutshell, for a perfected Raja yogi, thinking is a voluntary process all the time, unlike most of us who think of so many things involuntarily. We think about the pros and cons of every issue, even if we do not want to think of them. This is the uncontrolled nature of the mind. Raja-yoga is the process for attempting to control it. However, though this system of yoga was practiced in previous ages, in this age of Kali-Yuga, known for a predominance of confusion, pollution, quarrel and distractions, it is not an easy process nor the most recommended.

The Patanjali *Yoga-Sutras* consist of 196 slokas. In his book, Patanjali has never stated or mentioned that this is the only way for God-realization, so the proper state of mind as well as God-realization which he expounds can also be achieved by other religious practices.

Raja-Yoga incorporates eight steps of discipline to reach its goal, which are Yama, Niyama, Asana, Pranayama, Pratyahara, Dharana, Dhyana, and Samadhi. These are briefly defined as follows:

Yama—Abstinence from all vices.

Niyama—Observance of purity, contentment, etc.

Asana—a posture suitable for meditation.

Pranayama—consists of prolonged expiration (Rechaka); Inspiration (Purakha); and Retention (Kumbhaka) of breath. This exercise is supposed to be done only under the proper guidance of a realized master or guru. In the Pranayama exercise, the devotee is supposed to control the vital currents in the body.

Pratyahara—means retraction or withdrawal of our senses from contemplating sense-objects.

Dharana—fixing of mind on any object, preferably the Divine.

Dhyana–meditation on the Divine.

Samadhi—the final state. He who meditates perfectly can attain Samadhi. In that state, the mind loses its complete identity and assumes a formless state, even though it can assume the form of any object upon which it contemplates. In this stage of Samadhi, it is expected that the devotee realizes the ultimate truth.

Bhakti-yoga. This is one of the easiest Yoga paths to follow or practice, and is especially recommended for this age of Kali-Yuga. Most devotees of all religions who are sincere in their devotion to God are Bhakti-yogis, whether they believe in Hinduism or not. But Vedic culture is the only religion that explains these four paths of yoga in detail, especially the path of Bhakti or devotion. The process of developing one's love for God can reach a much deeper level of understanding and experience in the Vedic system than ever described in any western or conventional form of religion.

The word *bhakti* comes from the root word *bhaj*, which means "to be attached to". The *bhakti* relationship between man and God can be developed in six different forms:

1.   Madhura Bhava (amorous love);

2.   Kanta Bhava (love of wife for husband);

3.   Shanta Bhava (love of child for parent);

4.   Vatsalya Bhava (love of parent for child);

5.   Sakhya Bhava (friendship);

6.   Dasya Bhava (affection of servant for his master).

Hardly anywhere else but in the Vedic tradition are these forms of devotion explained so elaborately. There are many instructions and insights given for one to cultivate and develop such devotional and spiritually loving relations with God.

One of the great exponents of Bhakti-yoga was the sage Narada. Narada states in his book *Narada Bhakti Sutra*: "A man who loves God has no wants nor any sorrows. He neither hates nor survives with a zeal for any ends of his own. Through devotion he attains peace and is ever happy in spirit." In the highest aspect of *Bhakti-yoga*, the devotee goes for "total Self-surrender to the will of

God." All devotional books including the *Bhagavad-gita* advocate this type of Self-surrender. Lord Krishna promises in the *Bhagavad-gita* that He himself will take the burden of taking care of the day-to-day problems of a devotee who has dedicated himself to God by surrendering his free will. This promise of God is repeated many times in the *Gita*, in different *slokas*. The theme of total Self-surrender is often repeated in the Holy Bible, Koran, and other devotional religions.

Like other yogas, in Bhakti-yoga the final goal is liberation. But in Bhakti-yoga, regaining one's loving relationship with Lord Krishna is so ecstatic that it outweighs mere liberation from the pains and troubles of material existence. It provides a bliss that knows no bounds, if one dives deeply into it. Thus, it becomes the primary goal in Bhakti-yoga.

Great exponents of Bhakti-yoga include several great saints who practiced it in India. A few of the very prominent and contemporary ones are: Sri Chaitanya, Tulasi Das, Meera Bai, the Six Gosvamis of Vrindavana, and many others.

Mantra-yoga is another important form of yoga that is used in addition to the other major paths. It originated from the *Vedas* and *Tantras*. It is explained in the Vedic texts that in this age of Kali-yuga the process of chanting *japa* or mantra meditation is much more effective than practicing other spiritual paths that include meditating on the void or Brahman effulgence, or trying to control the life air within the body as in Raja-yoga. Only a very few can become perfect at such things as raising the *kundalini* force up through the various *chakras*, or moving the life air up to the top of the head for full enlightenment and then have it leave the body at the right time to achieve liberation. And meditating on the void becomes useless as soon as there is the slightest distraction, which in this age of Kali-yuga is a continuous thing. Therefore, the most effective means of focusing the consciousness is to concentrate on the sound vibration of a mantra.

Mantra-yoga brings about changes in material consciousness by the agency of sound as found in the Vedic mantras and verses. Of course, the "sound" that is referred to in Mantra-yoga is the transcendental sound which you cannot hear merely by the human ear. It goes deeper to the soul. From modern science, we know three important facts: 1. Matter is an expression of energy. 2. This energy vibrates at different frequencies in different types of matter. 3. Our sense-organs can only receive sensations made in a very limited frequency-range. For example, we can hear only the sound produced in a limited-frequency range and anything above this range is called Ultra Sound. The sound below that range is called Infra Sound. Of course, by no means can one conclude that the sound in Mantra-Yoga belongs to one of the categories above. We could say that Mantra-yoga is based on the vibratory aspect of energy and its modifications into varied matter. Mantras are specific sound formulas that are used to bring about substantial results as well as the unification and unfolding of consciousness.

Mantra-yoga as such is not an exclusive form of yoga. Instead it is widely used by devotees who practice all other forms of yoga for spiritual upliftment and the unfolding of consciousness. Mantra-yoga is actually a mystical tradition found in almost every spiritual path in the world. It may involve the softly spoken repetition of a prayer or mantra for one's own meditation, or it may be the congregational singing of spiritually uplifting songs, prayers, or the sacred names of God. It all involves the same process, but in the Eastern tradition it is called Mantra-yoga because it is the easy process of focusing our minds on the Supreme through His names, which helps spiritualize our consciousness.

In the word *mantra, man* means the mind, *tra* means deliverance. Therefore, a spiritual mantra is the pure sound vibration for delivering the mind from material to spiritual consciousness. This is the goal of any spiritual path. The premise in Mantra-yoga, especially in this age of Kali-yuga, is that instead of trying to void the mind of all thought or sensual stimuli so one can get a glimpse of the higher dimension, with mantra-yoga you simply fill the mind with the holy vibration of the mantra. So rather than emptying the mind we fill it with the higher and sacred object of our meditation, which is much easier for this age of Kali-yuga. Although all spiritual traditions have their own prayers or mantras, the Vedic mantras are especially powerful and effective in uniting us with the spiritual realm. However, a complete yoga process is generally a blend of a few yoga systems, such as Bhakti-yoga with Mantra-yoga. Therefore, Bhakti-yoga also includes Mantra-yoga, or the process of concentrating on the sound vibration within a mantra. This is especially important in this age of Kali.

The mantra is thus a point of meditation for the mind, but also a formula or transcendental sound vibration, like the holy name of God that releases its energy into one's consciousness. Thus it prepares one for perceiving higher states of reality. With constant practice of the appropriate mantra, and with the proper pronunciation and devotional mood, the mantra can reveal the Absolute Truth to the practitioner as well as one's spiritual form and the relationship that you have with the Supreme Being.

THE SIGNIFICANCE OF OM

One of the most often chanted mantras that you will hear in India is *Om*. It is chanted separately or quite often at the start of other mantras. It is known to have a profound effect on the body and mind of the chanter, and even on the surroundings. It is used at the start of auspicious activities, meditated on, or even used as a greeting with "Om", or "Hari Om".

It is also made of the letters AUM. There is a separate science in the way to use it in meditation. Briefly, it represents the three states of consciousness (waking, dream and deep sleep), the Vedic trinity (Brahma, Vishnu and Shiva), the three main *Vedas* (*Rig*, *Yajur* and *Sama*), and the three worlds (Bhuh, Bhuvah and Svaha), as well as the beginning, middle and end of all that exists. Om is also called the *pranava*, which means that by which the Lord is praised. It is a name of God as well as the vibration that pervades the universe. By meditating on Om properly, one can enter the realm of transcendence to the highest Truth. But the proper way of focusing the mind and meditating on Om is not as easy as one may think. There are particular rules to follow and methods of pronunciation that must be learned. There are numerous benefits by chanting Om, but without understanding the proper procedure, the inner potency of the mantra is not so easily invoked.

THE POTENCY OF THE HARE KRISHNA MANTRA

There are two mantras that are especially recommended in the Vedic literature. One is *omkara* or the *om* mantra, and the other is the *maha-mantra*, or the Hare Krishna mantra. It is explained that these two mantras can deliver one to the realm beyond material existence. The mantra that is especially meant to be chanted in this age is easy and is actually more directly connected with the Supreme than the sound vibration of *omkara* because it contains the direct holy names of the Lord. So the mantra for the age of Kali-yuga is the *maha-mantra*, or great mantra for deliverance, which is Hare Krishna, Hare Krishna, Krishna Krishna, Hare Hare/Hare Rama, Hare Rama, Rama Rama, Hare Hare. As it is said in the Vedic texts:

"These sixteen words—Hare Krishna, Hare Krishna, Krishna Krishna, Hare Hare/Hare Rama, Hare Rama, Rama Rama, Hare Hare—are especially meant for counteracting the ill effects of the present age of quarrel and anxiety." (*Kali-sant-arana Upanishad*)

"All mantras and all processes for self-realization are compressed into the Hare Krishna *maha-mantra*." (*Narada-pancaratra*)

"Chant the holy names, chant the holy names, chant the holy names. In this age of Kali [the age of quarrel and confusion] without a doubt there is no other way, there is no other way, there is no other way." (*Brihan-naradiya Purana* 38.126)

The reason that chanting the Lord's names is such an effective process is because the Lord and His names are identical: they are the same spiritual energy. By chanting Hare Krishna we are in immediate contact with God. If we chant someone else's name, we cannot enjoy their association because the name and the person are different. For example, by chanting "water, water, water," we do not quench our thirst because water and the name are two different things. But in the spiritual world everything is absolute. Krishna is nondifferent from His names and, therefore, we can feel His presence simply by chanting His names. This is further elaborated in the *Caitanya-caritamrta* (*Madhya-lila*, 17.131-133), which explains that there is no difference between the Lord's name, form, or personality, and they are all transcendentally sweet. Krishna's name is the same as Krishna Himself and is not material in any way. It gives spiritual benedictions and is full of pleasure. But in the material world everything is different. Furthermore, in *Caitanya-caritamrta* (*Adi-lila*, 17.22, and the *Padma Purana*), the Hare Krishna *maha-mantra* is said to be the sound incarnation of Krishna, and anyone who chants this mantra is in direct association with Krishna and is delivered from the clutches of the material energy.

8

Particular Traits Of Vedic/
Hindu Worship

This section explains some of the common characteristics about the nature and traditions of worship in the Vedic system that are followed by many Dharmists or Hindus. In the Vedic culture of Sanatana-dharma, everything has a purpose and meaning behind it, and reason why it is done. Thus, we merely need to understand the meaning behind the customs.

WHY HINDUS WORSHIP IMAGES

The use of images is an integral part of religious practice as can be seen in a variety of faiths, such as the Catholic, Greek Orthodox Christianity, Native American, African, and numerous other native religions. Only Protestant Christianity and Muslims deny the use of images and claim it as idolatry, yet they also use pictures, crosses, or the black rock and the place of Mecca as holy symbols. However, it is surprising when certain religions claim that their use of images is sacred but they say the use of them by Hindus is evil.

Almost any person [except maybe Jews] believes or utilizes an image or symbol of their religion, culture, or even business. This is not unusual. The Cross in the Christian church, the picture of Jesus Christ, the statue of Mary, statues of patron saints, even the black stone in the Kabba are all what we could call images. However, one could say that if anyone bows in front of any of them, they are breaking laws of the Old Testament. [LE 26:1, and EX 20:2-5.] Nonetheless, use of images is everywhere and all people worship something or someone. In fact, the first sculpture of Christ was in the form of a small boy holding a lamb. Now, everywhere in the world people have pictures of Christ according to their culture. It may be a loving, young, white man in the USA, or a tough man looking like a judge in Russia, a nice black man in Africa, and you find a man looking like a typical Chinese with a sheepish beard in China. All religions have some concept of God with name and form, but Hindus have the courage to present the details as described in their scripture.

Hindus do not worship stone or metal images as God. They invoke God into the image through special rites and worship God through that image, as described in Vedic Shastra. This is God's mercy on us to see what is spiritual through material senses. Thus, even if someone says the deity is only stone or metal, or made of material elements, those elements are still the energy of God and thus an extension of the Lord's energy. Furthermore, the images and deities of the Divine that are worshiped in the Vedic temples or in homes of those who follow Sanatana-dharma are not someone's concocted imaginings. They are based on the detailed descriptions of God's form as described in the Vedic texts. This is another beauty of the Vedic culture. Whereas most texts of other religions offer little information on God's appearance and characteristics, these become specifically revealed in the Vedic tradition. Thus, we know what God looks like and can form images accordingly. Then these deities are installed according to specific prayers and rituals to call the personality of the Divine.

As the Supreme Controller, God can appear to His devotees in any of His specific forms. And even if some say that these images that are presented are made of nothing but stone or wood, still God can turn what is spiritual into something material, or something material into something spiritual. In this way, we can use our material senses and still have the vision of God in the form of the deity, and approach Him with our love and service. Thus, the authorized deity is not an idol, but is the Lord's mercy in giving us the chance to see something spiritual with material eyes. Of course, as we become more spiritualized, we can see with our inner spiritual eyes the transcendental form and activities of the Supreme Being, even while in this body that we have now.

An example is that the Post Office has authorized post boxes in which we put our mail, which is then picked up and delivered to the address on the envelope. If, however, we make our own unauthorized box and put it where we like, if we put our mail in it, it will not go anywhere. In the same way, by praying to the authorized forms of God our service will reach Him and be accepted by Him. Besides, there are many stories of how deities have come to life and interacted with devotees and engaged in all kinds of pastimes with them in very personal ways. So they are always full of potential to interact with us, or merely watch and see what we do, or even leave the deity form if we are too offensive or do not understand the basis of the deity. So we should never think that deities are nothing but stone or wood. In fact, the Vedic scripture says that anyone who thinks in such a way exhibits a hellish mentality.

HINDUS DO NOT WORSHIP IDOLS

First of all, the word "idol" is an English term that is often meant in a derogatory way in reference to a false god or form. There is no Sanskrit equivalent for that term. *Murti* is the Sanskrit terminology for a form or shape of a personality or divine being. We can also use the term "deity" in this way. Idolatry means the worship of a false god, or the worship of something that is material. The worship of money is equivalent to idolatry.

The *murti* may often exhibit multiple arms or heads, all of which are meant to show the diverse powers of the personality. Multiple hands holding various weapons or instruments are meant to reveal the many kinds of potencies that the Divinity possesses. Every aspect of the *murti* has meaning and makes a statement about the divine nature of the personality if we can understand the meaning of it. That is why the Vedic *shastra* has so much information that can help enlighten us in this way.

Worship of the deity is a way of cultivating devotion to God in the form of the *murti*, which is the form of God that we can see with our material eyes. Thus, by forming the image according to the descriptions in the *shastra* and then calling God by sacred ritual to enter the form of the deity, then by His causeless mercy He appears in a way that we can view Him with our material senses. Otherwise, we would need our consciousness to be completely spiritualized if we were to get the chance to see God on the spiritual platform. But if God enters the deity to accept our service, then we can also enter the state of consciousness wherein we have *darshan* of the Lord. *Darshan* is that state in which there is a loving exchange between God and ourselves when we see God and God also sees us. Thus, our minds and devotion become ever more increased and focused on God.

Rituals performed in respect and worship to the *murti* is to allow a way to express and offer our love to God. This may include offering fire lamps, fans, sandal paste, food, etc. Worship offered to the deities is a way of showing and developing love, honor and service to God. Even simple items can be offered with love and Lord Krishna says He will accept it. (*Bhagavad-gita* 9:26) So it is not the expense of the offering or the opulence that makes the difference, but it is only the love that is accepted, and with love He accepts our offering. Thus, you could say that God accepts our love over anything else. It is not the significance of the object that is offered, but it is the intention and attitude with which the offering is made. Thus, the offering and worship is an expression of the love we have to offer, which is actualized by our thoughts, devotion and the service we render to God and His parts and parcels, the other living beings. This is what draws us closer to God and what attracts God closer to us. It is the way the finite, by submissive service, attracts the Infinite.

BASIC TECHNIQUES IN VEDIC WORSHIP OF GOD

Worshiping God in Sanskrit is *puja*, the act of worship or adoration. Worship can be done on a personal or private level, or as *mahapujas*, meaning with a great number of participants. This is often the case with large festivals on great holy days.

Among the forms of expression in one's worship, *prarthana* or prayer is a common technique on the Dharmic path. It is used as a way to communicate with God in a personal way for asking for blessings, assistance, or for expressing repentance for a misdeed, or in sincerely praising God. It is also a form of worship and meditation. However, prayer can be found in many other forms as well.

There is also *Smarana* or the means of focusing our minds on the Lord, especially in remembering God and His pastimes as described in the Vedic texts, particularly the *Puranas*. In that way we can recount His glories, character, strength, personality, beauty and grace. This also can be done through the repetition of one's favorite mantra.

Kirtan or singing the glories and nature of God in the form of songs and *bhajans* is another method to accomplish this. It is also an affective form of meditation to sing the glories of God for oneself, or to use musical instruments and join with others to sing beautiful songs of love for God. Large numbers of people can join in and create a soul-stirring experience for all who participate. This is always a means of purifying one's consciousness and heightening one's devotion and spiritual awareness.

There is also *Archana* or the ritual used in the worship of the Lord. *Atma nivedana* or inner dialogue and reflection is another means for concentrating on God and one's connection and devotion to God.

WHY DEVOTEES HAVE PRAYER ROOMS IN THEIR HOUSE

Many devotees and Hindus will make space for a prayer room in their homes. These are meant to have their own sacred atmosphere and will contain holy pictures, prints, utensils, deities or images, lamps and burning incense. Nothing is to be done in this room without a spiritual purpose. Thus, the atmosphere in the room never becomes contaminated by any other activity or selfish consciousness. It has its own special atmosphere. Thus, it becomes a means to get away from everything else, or free from the common thoughts of the day. In this way, it is easy to enter into meditation or engage in chanting *japa* for mantra meditation or worship of the deity, offering prayers, or sing *bhajans* without other thoughts causing distractions. Such a room also indicates that the Supreme is the proprietor of the house, and our very lives, whom we respect and honor in this way. Therefore, this is the way that we continue to live our spiritual life whether we go to a local temple or not because we have made our own house into a temple. So we commune with God and invoke His grace everyday and on special occasions in the prayer or temple room of our house.

WHAT IS "NAMASTE"

This is the popular greeting performed by pressing two hands together and holding them near the heart and bowing slightly while saying "Namaste". The whole act communicates to the world the spiritual significance that "You and I are one", or "I salute and worship the God within you, which is a mirror image of myself". It is also called *namaskar*, which is understood as salutations or prostration, and a way of paying homage to each other. Its spiritual significance is the negation or reduction of one's ego in the presence of another.

The bowing of the head is a gracious form of extending friendship in love, respect and humility. Adding spiritual devotion to this gesture is done when we also add such sacred words as, "Namaste", "Hare Krishna", "Jai Sri Krishna", "Radhe Radhe", "Jai Sri Rama", "Hari Om", "Namo Narayana", "Om Shanti", "Om Namah Shivaya", etc. These words are actually paying respect to the Divine, and certain sayings are often preferred in particular places. Thus, the Namaste gesture with these words does not remain a superficial gesture but provides a deeper communication and meaning between one another.

WHY RED DOTS ARE WORN ON THE FOREHEAD

The red dot on the forehead represents divine sight into higher realms and dimensions of who we are. Thus, it represents the opening of the third eye of inner vision. It indicates the vision or the reminder of the vision a person should have to see our real identity as spiritual beings that reside in these material bodies. When men wear such dots, which are often applied with the finger tip, it is often because they have visited a temple, or are worshipers of Devi, in which case it is a sign of their devotion and that the body is a temple. You will also find that many Hindu ladies wear red dots on their foreheads as a sign of being married, just as Christians wear wedding rings. It may be worn daily or on special occasions, or while going to the temple. This is called *kumkum*, and is often made from dyed rice flour.

WHAT IS TILOK OR FOREHEAD MARKS

The *tilok* marks that may be seen on devotees and Hindu saints are usually in two forms: applied in a V shape in the center of the forehead, or as three lines applied horizontally across the forehead. It will vary in design according to the sect of the person. A simple *tilok* in the V shape may be white or dark, using *chandan* or clay from certain holy places, or sandalwood paste. These indicate that one is a Vaishnava, or worshiper of Vishnu and Krishna. Or it may have a red streak down the center that indicates that one is a worshiper of Lord Rama. Or it may be the three-lined sacred ash, called *bhasma*, streaked horizontally across the forehead that indicates one is a Shaivite, or worshiper of Shiva. A simple red dot is also worn by those who worship Devi. Other shapes and colors will indicate other purposes. Sometimes you may even see a holy man whose entire forehead is covered with *chandan* or *bhasma tilok*.

Such marks may be applied as part of the morning ritual or custom with a mantra or prayer. A small portion of *kumkum* or *chandan* may be offered by a temple priest to the guests who visit the temple after it has been offered to the deity. Among other things that it indicates is that it marks the body as a temple, a vehicle with the soul and Supersoul within. So it helps invoke a feeling of sanctity in the wearer, and reminds others of the spiritual significance of who we are. The *tilok* also covers the spot between the eyebrows which is the seat of memory, thinking and the third eye, or spiritual center of consciousness, the Ajna Chakra. The *tilok* is said to help activate that center. It is also said to help cool the forehead against heat generated from worry that may also cause headaches. Thus, it protects us from energy loss. However, the *tilok* marks are also applied to other parts of the body, such as the arms, chest, and back, all of which are to indicate the sacredness of the soul within the body, or the holy aspect of the body when it is used in the service of the Lord.

WHAT IS THE HOLY ASH

The holy ash, *bhasma*, is not any ordinary ash, but it is the remnants from the *homa* or sacred fire into which special wood, ghee and other herbs have been offered as worship of the Divine. *Homa* also signifies the offering of the ego and material desires into the flame of knowledge. Sometimes the deity is worshiped with ash which is then distributed as *bhasma*. So the ash, that is applied to the forehead as well as other parts of the body, indicates purity of mind, or the attempt to attain it. It also indicates the destruction of the false identity of the body which brings freedom from birth and death. Some ascetics, such as austere

Shaivites, will rub it all over the body. This also keeps the body somewhat warm, especially for the Naga Babas who may wear little or no clothing, but undergo whatever nature brings their way. Shiva also smeared it all over his body. When the ash is applied to the forehead with a red dot in the center, it indicates a unity of the Shiva-Shakti principle.

The word *bhasma* means "that by which our sins are destroyed and the Lord is remembered". So it indicates the destruction of evil and the invocation of the Divine. It is also called *vibhuti* (which means glory) and *raksha* (which means source of protection).

WHY IS SHANTI SAID THREE TIMES

Shanti means peace, a natural state of being that everyone wishes to reach. Peace is naturally experienced when all agitations end. The most important peace is to attain it within the mind, internally. So in many mantras, or at the end of many prayers, *shanti* is said three times because it is believed that anything said three times with enough focus or concentration will manifest. It is also to emphasize something. So when *shanti* is chanted three times, we first say it loudly, then softer, and then more softly.

WHY RING BELLS IN TEMPLES

When entering a temple, most of them have one or more bells hung from the ceiling. The devotee rings the bells as he or she enters, then proceeds for *darshan* to see the deities. The ring of the bell produces a sound similar to *Om*, the universal name of the Lord. This helps create an atmosphere of auspiciousness when entering the temple. This is also a reason why a bell is rung by a priest, *pujari*, while doing the *arati* ceremony. Ringing the bell, blowing the conch, and engaging in the *kirtanas* or singing holy songs, are all ways to worship the Lord and keep away all inauspicious and irrelevant noises and thoughts that might disturb or distract the worshipers from their devotions and inner peace.

THE REASON LAMPS ARE USED

In many homes and temples there are lamps that are lit. And many special functions start with the lighting of a lamp. Light symbolizes knowledge which keeps us free from the darkness of ignorance. Knowledge removes ignorance just as light removes darkness. Therefore, the lamp is lit and we bow to it as this knowledge is the greatest form of wealth. It is kept lit during special functions as a guide and witness to our thoughts and actions. Of course, now lamps are not as necessary with the use of electric bulbs, etc. But the lamp is the traditional instrument which represents our *vasanas* or negative inclinations, while the wick signifies our ego. As the lamp burns, it also represents the burning away of our bad habits and bodily ego. The flame burns upward, as knowledge also takes our views higher.

THE SIGNIFICANCE OF THE AARATI CEREMONY

The *aarati* ceremony, as when it is used in the process of *bhakti* or devotional yoga, is also a process of engaging the soul in direct service to the Lord through the use of the body. The ritual is thus completely spiritual and therefore beyond time and space. So in that condition, the soul of the person engaged in the ritual and all souls observing it have the potential of rising above the material energy and its influence. In this way, it provides the observer to become emmersed in the spiritual atmosphere and one's relationship with God. Thus, the ritual is the means for the soul to go beyond time and place, reaching a completely transcendental state.

The *aarati* ceremony is the offering of a ghee lamp to the deity or object of respect. These lamps usually have five or more flames on them. *Aarati* is performed in the temples to the deities several times a day. It is also offered to special guests and holy saints. It is also accompanied with ringing a bell along with singing or playing musical instruments.

Camphor is also used in place of ghee at times. This is usually a single flame in the lamp from a piece of burning camphor. This also presents a pleasing scent. The ghee or camphor also represents our inherent tendencies that are being offered to the fire of knowledge, which reveals the form of the Lord and thus increases our mental and physical purity in service to the Lord.

In offering the lamp to the deity, it is held in the right hand and waved in a clockwise motion, 4 times to the feet, 2 times to the waist, 3 times to the head, and 7 times around the whole body. We use the lamp to light the form of the Lord who is in fact the source of all light. This was particularly significant before there was electricity and when temples were lit by lamps. The *aarati* ceremony would especially provide light to various parts of the deity when the priest would wave the lamp in front of it. Some of the older temples in India are still like this today. It is also a way of adding intensity to the prayers and the image of the Lord as we meditate on each limb of the Lord. Besides, the aroma of the burning ghee is quite pleasing, which is another reason why we offer this to the deity. Afterwards, the ghee lamp is passed around the room so that everyone can place their hands over the flame that has been offered to the deity, accepting it as holy remnants called *prasada*, and then we touch our hands to our eyes or head. This is a gesture of accepting the light of knowledge, and the light which revealed the Lord, and raising our hands that have touched the flame to our forehead as a sign that it may light our own vision and thoughts and that they may be divine and noble.

WHY A CONCH SHELL IS BLOWN

Whether in temples or in our household temple rooms, the conch shell is blown three times before the *aarati* ceremony or *puja*, worship. It is kept on the altar as a symbol for Truth, *dharma*, auspiciousness, and victory. It also was blown before a battle or after the victory of an army. Blowing the conch emanates the sound of Om, which contains all the knowledge of the *Vedas*. It is an auspicious sound and represents the truth behind the illusion. It also can purify the atmosphere, as well as the minds of those who hear it. It also represents *dharma* or righteousness. So it is appropriate for it to be blown before the *aarati* or *puja*. The sound of the conch draws one's attention to the presence of the Lord and the Vedic sound vibration. It thus drowns out the negative noises that may distract us from the sacred atmosphere or disturb our minds. This is also why sometimes devotees bow to the sound of the conch when it is blown.

The tradition relates that there was once a demon named Shankhasura who had defeated the *devas* (demigods) and stole the *Vedas* from them. He then hid at the bottom of the ocean. The *devas* prayed to Lord Vishnu for assistance. He incarnated as Matsya and killed the demon. The Lord blew one of the conch shells that hung from His ears and the Om resonated, from which the *Vedas* returned. For this reason the conch is also called *shankha* after Shankhasura. The Lord's conch shell is named Panchajanya.

WHY COCONUTS ARE OFFERED

One of the most common items that are offered to the deities in the temple is the coconut. You will also see it being used to start special occasions, like weddings, festivals, etc., when it is offered and then broken. You may also see it sitting on top of a pot with mango leaves. This is a representation of Lakshmi devi, the goddess of fortune, or sometimes Lord Shiva. The coconut is offered to the deity as a representation of the body (the coconut shell), mind (the white fruit within) and soul (the milk). All these are offered to the deity, and then it is broken to let out the milk and fruit. This indicates the breaking of the ego. Then, after it is offered to the Lord, what remains is accepted as remnants from the Lord, as *prasada*. This represents a complete circle in which God accepts our offering of the body, mind and soul and gives back the mercy, *prasada*, of the Lord.

PURPOSE OF OFFERING FOOD TO THE LORD BEFORE EATING

We often see that food preparations are offered to the deities during the worship. Or even in homes of devotees, food is prepared and then offered to the deities in the family temple room before anyone else accepts it. Then it is taken as *prasada* or mercy of the deities or God as spiritualized food. Even in many western homes food is taken only after observing a prayer. This is a recognition that whatever blessings we receive in life is a result of the Lord's arrangement. After all, everything is God's property, and we are merely borrowing it. So we offer to God whatever we accept before taking it ourselves which then purifies it. We can especially do this with food.

Furthermore, it has been detected that the particles of food change when prayers are said over it. So offering the food to God increases the high level of energy that goes into it that would otherwise not be there. And then we honor the offered and purified food by respectfully eating it. This further purifies and spiritualizes our own body, mind and consciousness which helps pave the way for increased spiritual progress.

WHY A KALASHA (POT) IS WORSHIPED

Sometimes, especially during a *homa* ritual, there is a special pot or *kalasha* topped with a coconut that is given special attention. The pot may be made from brass, copper or mud, and filled with water. Tied around its neck may be a red and white string. The pot often has designs on its sides. It may be used for special occasions like weddings, or set near entrances of homes, etc. The water in the *kalasha* symbolizes the waters of creation when the cosmic manifestation appeared with the arrangements of Lord Vishnu and Brahma. The leaves and coconut represent the creation, while the string indicates the love that is the foundation of the whole creation. When prayers are offered to the *kalasha*, it is considered that all the holy waters, the Vedic knowledge, and the blessings of the deities are invoked in it. The purified water within is then used in the rituals. At other times, the prayers are used to invoke the energy of the Goddess of Fortune, Lakshmi Devi, and the *kalasha* becomes a representation of Lakshmi.

WHY WORSHIP THE TULASI TREE

Respect for plants and the resources that we depend on is a basic premise of the Vedic culture. In fact, one of the ways of doing social service is to plant trees for shade along the paths that people regularly use. Another point is to use only as much of the plants or trees that is needed, whether it be for food, shelter or fuel. Indeed, cutting trees unnecessarily is considered a sin or way of accumulating bad karma. So respect for trees is naturally a part of the Vedic path. In fact, some trees have such good medicinal qualities and benefits that they remain highly regarded till this day.

However, there are some specific plants that are given more respect for particular reasons. The *tulasi* tree is very special. It is not unusual to find it in many temples in India in the courtyard, or even in homes. In fact, it is considered a part of worship to take care of it, water it and circumambulate it. The whole plant, and even its soil, is considered sacred. A leaf from the *tulasi* plant is placed on the food that is offered to Lord Vishnu or Krishna. It is His favorite tree. The *tulasi* is considered an incarnation or expansion of a pure devotee of the Lord. This is based on a long traditional story in the Vedic literature. She also symbolizes Goddess Lakshmi, and once a year there is the festival of the marriage ceremony between *tulasi* and the Lord. This is because the Lord also blessed her to be His consort. So the worship of the *tulasi* tree is a part of the devotional service to Lord Krishna and Vishnu.

WHY THE LOTUS IS SACRED

The lotus, besides being India's national flower, is a symbol of truth, beauty and auspiciousness. The Lord is also compared with these principles and its beauty. You can easily find it in many parts of India adorning ponds and lakes. The lotus grows out of the water but raises above it. It remains beautiful and untainted regardless from where it grows. In this way, it shows that we too can remain unaffected by the world of trouble and doubt around us. The Vedic literature has numerous references to the beauty of the lotus, and it is a common architectural motif. Lord Vishnu and Goddess Lakshmi both carry a lotus in their hands. A lotus also emerged from the navel of Lord Vishnu during the process of universal creation, from which Brahma originated. Thus, the lotus also indicates the link between the Creator and the creation. So the lotus is highly regarded.

PURPOSE OF FASTING

Dharmic devotees sometimes fast on certain days. This sort of fasting is called *Upavaasa*, which means to stay near. This is in regard to staying near the Lord in mental disposition by spending more time in thought of God without using the time and energy in procuring items of food to prepare, cook and eat. Food does certain things to us according to its quality. Some of it will heighten our awareness while other types may indeed make our minds clouded and dull. So on special days, a devotee may save time and conserve energy by either eating very simple and light foods, or even by not eating at all. Thus, one's mind can remain alert and absorbed in thoughts of God, and not be pre-occupied thinking of what to eat.

On a more mundane level, it is also a way of giving the body and digestive system a break, and letting it get cleaned out. Fasting also helps bring control and discipline over the senses and calms our mind. However, fasting for some other reason based on ego or politics will not bring the same results. And one should not become unnecessarily weak by long fasts. This can become counterproductive in keeping the mind and senses equipoised for developing meditative spiritual awareness and love for God if we become too weak, or focused only on desiring food to eat. Lord Krishna advises us in the *Bhagavad-gita* that we should take the middle path of not eating too much nor too little, but to eat purely, simply and healthily for keeping body and soul together for spiritual purposes.

PURPOSE OF TEMPLES

Vedic temples are often ornate and beautifully carved with images of the Divine and many other aspects of life adorning the exterior. They may also have numerous paintings of rulers who helped establish the temple, or of saintly men of the tradition, or the tales from the Vedic legends and stories. Temples are like the center and preservers of the culture. Many Hindus go to the local temple everyday, or a few times during the week. The temples are an expression of all forms of community life, but with emphasis on the Divine. Rituals of all kinds are performed in the temples, from regular worship to weddings to blessings of children, or for those who have died.

Many people also give much money to temples for their upkeep and worship as a service to God. Others may give items such as fruits, grains, vegetables or ghee for the offerings to the deities in the temple. This is considered a way of using their life as a service to the Divine, and thus a way of meditating on the Divine in the temple while going about their daily work, shopping, or other activities. Holy festivals are often observed there, which may include music and dance as well.

The architecture of the temple is also styled in a way to mirror the universe and its forces. It is like the launching pad from which a person can more appropriately meditate and reach God. However, a temple can be quite simple as well, noted mostly for the sacred atmosphere inside that helps one focus on the Divine and the purpose of life. Thus, a temple is very important for most Hindus.

In essence temples:

1. Help preserve the Dharmic traditions

2. Are the hubs of social, religious and cultural life for the communities.

3. Help set examples for the next generation of Hindus and are a facility to provide for their education of the Vedic way of life and the purpose of it.

4. Where the priests are the principle custodians of Dharmic traditions.

5. Help present the value, knowledge and education of the Dharmic way of life to non-Hindus, and explain the purpose, meaning and philosophy behind the rituals and holy festivals.

6. Help preserve and explain the meaning of the Vedic scripture, legends, and histories.

7. Help preserve Sanskrit and the original religious texts.

8. Provide a place where the performance of *pujas*, rituals, festivals, *samskaras*, and traditional dances can be held.

9. Must also help in the problems of the members of the Hindu community and provide confidential advisors for such problems of all sorts.

THE SIGNIFICANCE OF THE VEDIC TEMPLE

The Vedic temple is steeped in significance and meaning. The most important part of the temple is the inner sanctum, called the Garbhagriha, in which the main deity is housed. The Shukanasi and Antarala are the adjoining passages that connect with the Navaranga or Mandapa hallway, which serves as the main hall for the religious activities and the congregating of the people who visit the temple. This is also where the pilgrims and visitors will engage in *sankirtana*, or the congregational chanting of the mantras and singing of the sacred texts and hymns, and the names of the Lord. Near the mandapa is the stambha or flagpost, which carries the insignia of the main deity like a flag. There is often the Balipitha or pedestal for offerings that is also near the sanctum. The larger temples will often have smaller chambers or shrines for other divinities in the hallways or around the central sanctum to the main deity. Large temple compounds will also be surrounded by high walls known as the Prakara. The temple is often entered through a tall pyramidal tower called a gopuram, especially in the style of South India. This has the main door at the base, and smaller doors on each level up representing the doors of the successively higher beings.

The symbolism of a temple is that it represents the body of God. The Garbha-griha or sanctum indicates the head of the deity. While the gopuram or large gate wherein people enter the compound, at least for the larger temples, represents the feet of the Supreme Being. The Shukanasi is His nose while the Antaral, the narrow passage connecting the sanctum with the mandapa hall, is His neck. The Prakaras are positioned as His hands. Thus, a temple is like walking into the body of the Supreme Being, or like a vehicle to accelerate one's consciousness to increasingly higher realms of reality, not only by remembering the purpose of the form of the temple, but by the worship of the deities inside, and seeing the tall tower and paintings of the various Vedic divinities on the interior walls.

At special times, they may bring the temple *utsavar* deities, or smaller festival deities outside to ride on special *rathas* or carts. The carts are like moving temples. It is considered especially auspicious to see the deities ride on the carts since it represents the deity's special mercy to come outside to offer everyone the chance to have *darshan*, or the means to see the deity in a loving exchange. Thus, the appearance of the deity in such a way gives special grace and happiness.

When one visits the temple, they are expected to be physically clean and mentally focused with devotion. They should enter the temple with reverence, and quietly go toward the main sanctum while offering obeisances or respects to any deities that are along the path. Some temples will have shrines to Ganesh that you see before or on the way to the main sanctum. Ganesh removes all the obstacles and provides good luck, and in the temple he removes obstacles in one's devotion to God. So this provides the means to enhance one's endeavor to please and see the Lord and develop higher states of devotion. While in the sanctum, the priest may do some *puja* or worship on your behalf to the main deity. This may involve offering incense or a lit ghee lamp, or flowers and coconut or fruits and sweets. Afterward the priest will then often give back to you some of what has already been offered as *prasada*, or the Lord's mercy, which you then can honor by reverentially eating it. After this, one may exit the sanctum and then circumambulate the sanctum through the halls just outside of it. These often have other shrines to various divinities or paintings of the legends from the *Puranas* or Vedic histories. If not, then they may be located in other hallways in the temple structure.

PURPOSE OF CIRCUMAMBULATING TEMPLES OR DEITIES

Another thing that you may see is when devotees circumambulate and go around the deities in the sanctum of a temple, or even around the temple itself, or around sacred places, like special hills or even holy towns. This is called *pradakshina*. This is a means of recognizing the center point of our lives, the center of the circular path we take in honor of the deities of the Lord, or something connected with Him. This is done in a clockwise manner so to keep the deity on our right, which is the side of auspiciousness. So in a way, it is a reflection of going through life while keeping God in the center. Walking around holy sites is another way of undergoing austerities for spiritual merit. It is accepted that each step takes away some of our material karma, and thus helps us get free from the mundane affairs and worldly consciousness which causes us to undertake the actions which create our karma. This helps free us from further rounds of birth and death. Respect can be shown to our superiors or parents by circumambulating them three times as well.

WHY NON-HINDUS ARE NOT ALWAYS ALLOWED TO ENTER TEMPLES IN INDIA

This is an issue that has been coming to the fore of late, mostly because there is an increasing number of non-Indian born people who have taken up the Dharmic path and have learned the ways of the Vedic system. So why should they not be allowed into the temples to partake of their chosen religion or spiritual path? Such discrimination toward those who are devout in the Vedic system is unjustified. However, if those who are non-Hindus visit the temples with the same faith as when they visit their own churches or places of worship, then there is no harm and there should be no objection. Nonetheless, if they are merely coming into the temple with an attitude of a tourist, without faith or proper understanding and view things with an attitude of criticism or ridicule, then obviously this would not be appropriate. Neither would they be benefited and they would also spoil the atmosphere for others. But temples should be willing to admit all sincere Hindus into the temple if they are genuine followers of Santana-Dharma, regardless of what section of society they may come from.

PURPOSE OF PILGRIMAGES

As anyone knows, the usual routine of daily life can become lifeless and boring after a long time. Thus, taking time to go on pilgrimage to see the holy places and sacred temples will bring back the enthusiasm for life. Pilgrimage is viewed as a sacrifice of time and energy to travel to the holy places, but also a means to become recharged by visiting such holy venues for spiritual upliftment. It is like recharging one's batteries to endure the routine of ordinary life again. It also invokes in one the special nature of pursuing one's spiritual path, even while at home doing the normal routine. It is the holy places, called *dhamas*, wherein the spiritual atmosphere is especially apparent, and where the association with the temples, sages, and doing special *pujas* or worship can purify one's consciousness and view of life, and reinvigorate one's faith. Very often these places are associated with special historic events that are described in the *Puranas* and sacred Vedic texts. They also are known for being a place where the Lord may have appeared, or where the spiritual atmosphere is especially noticeable. Thus, they are spiritually surcharged and can help purify one and accelerate their spiritual progress. Because of this, such places also purify one of past sinful karma and take away things that may block his or her continued or rapid spiritual development.

A holy place is called a *tirtha*, and visiting or short stays at such places is a means of spiritual purification. The high spiritual vibrations that emanate at these holy *tirthas* can indeed have an effect on our own consciousness in most beneficial ways. Also, remembering the pastimes that may have taken place at such holy locations can also reveal the reality and authenticity of the Vedic legends and historical significance of the tradition.

There are different types of *tirthas* one may visit. There is the eternal holy site (*nitya tirtha*) where the spiritual dimension may overlap into the material world to provide us with additional benefit by visiting them. This may include places where the *avataras* of the Lord descended into the world to display spiritual pastimes to attract us. Such places may include Mathura, Dwaraka, Badrinatha, Ramesvaram, and others that mark places where the Lord appeared. When visiting these places it is common to spend time remembering the sacred pastimes that took place there. There are also places like the holy Ganga (Ganges) and Yamuna rivers, or mountains such as Mount Kailash in Tibet or Govardhana Hill in the holy town of Vrindavana.

Other types of holy sites are called *bhagavadiya tirthas*. These are the places where the Lord took birth or where the deities of the Lord appeared, or where other appearance pastimes took place. Vrindavana is the place where Lord Krishna appeared and Ayodhya is the place where Lord Rama manifested in the earthly realm. These are quite popular on the pilgrimage routes. The spiritual vibration and dimension that God radiates remains at these holy sites, so they are extremely divine and purifying for the pilgrim. Thus, they should be visited with utmost respect and humility, knowing that the Divine also stood at these very places. One other type of *tirtha* is the *sant tirtha*, or the places where the great devotees and saints reside.

WHY HINDUS RESPECT THE COW

It is sometimes said that Hindus worship the cow. However, they do not specifically worship the cow, but they respect all beings. The cow represents the mode of goodness and the generosity and giving disposition that all Hindus respect in life. Cows are a symbol of the Dharma. They are gentle and tolerant, and selflessly provide service to others. They are viewed as being one of our mothers since the cow supplies milk for the benefit of other creatures and for human consumption. The cow symbolizes the reciprocation between human society and nature, for which gratitude is an appropriate response. The cow is also Lord Krishna's favorite animal. Thus, there may be festivals in which the cow is decorated and respected in recognition of this giving nature. After all, the cow and bull only take a little grass or grain and give back so much in the form of labor, milk, inexpensive fuel, etc. The bull is viewed like a father since he helps plow the field to grow crops. The bull is still used on small farms in India and elsewhere for plowing fields or helping produce food through its working capacity. The cow's milk can also be made into cream, butter, yogurt, ghee, etc. from which many other preparations can be made. Because of this and many other reasons the cow is respected by all Vedic Dharmists. Thus, respect for the cow instills one with appreciation for the traits of gentleness and sensitivity, and for the benevolence that God provides through animals like the cow and bull. This is but a reflection of the care and protection that should be given toward all life, and the reverence and respect for the environment and nature.

9

The Dharmic Festivals

In the Vedic/Hindu tradition, there are many festivals that are observed throughout the year. There are major festivals and numerous minor ones, as well as those that are observed on a local or regional basis, which are celebrated differently according to the location, or even named differently. There are festivals to celebrate the various *avataras* of God, as well as those that honor the seasons, harvests, relationships, and certain principles of the Vedic culture, all of which allow people to readily apply the Vedic principles with enthusiasm, and taste the result of one's steady faith and dedication. Some of the major festivals are listed and described as follows:

Makara Sankranti: Hindus consider the Sun king of the planets. Makara Sankranti is the celebration of the sun's (Surya's) journey back toward the Northern Hemisphere when many people may do Surya *puja*. It is celebrated in mid-January. It is known as Lohri in the north in Punjab and Pongal in South India. It is celebrated with a feast that includes a dish made of green gram, rice and jaggery. People also may bathe in holy rivers.

Vasant Panchami: Vasant Panchami is known as the festival of kites. Many kites may be sold at this time. It is celebrated towards the end of winter in the month of January-February. Vasant Panchami is celebrated in the northern parts of India. The weather changes from harsh winter to soft spring or "Vasant". Vasant is the time when the mustard fields are abound with their yellow flowers that seem to usher in spring. So Punjabis welcome the change and celebrate the day by wearing yellow clothes, holding feasts and by organizing kite flying, especially amongst the children. Vasant Panchami day puja (worship) is devoted to Sarasvati, the Goddess of Learning. She bestows the greatest wealth to humanity—the wealth of knowledge.

Maha Shivaratri: Shivaratri is celebrated sometime during February-March. It is believed that Parvati, the wife of Shiva, prayed, meditated and fasted on this day for the well being of Shiva and hoped to ward off any evils that may fall upon him. Though both men and women celebrate Shivaratri, it is an especially auspicious day for women. Married women pray for the well being of their husbands and sons, while unmarried women pray for a husband like Shiva, who is considered to be the ideal husband.

On Shivaratri, devotees awake at sunrise and bathe in holy water (like the Ganges River) and wear new clothes. On the day of the festival, people will fast and spend the day focused on Shiva, meditating and chanting "Om Namaha Shivaya". Thus, offering their obeisances to Lord Shiva, the mind is held in such single-pointed concentration throughout the day. Then they flock to the temples carrying holy water to bathe and worship the Shiva lingam. This bathing of the Shiva lingam symbolizes the cleansing of one's soul. Next, the Shiva lingam is decorated with flowers and garlands. It is customary to spend the entire night awake singing the praises of Lord Shiva.

Shivaratri is a festival that is held in the typical pattern of preparation, purification, realization, and then celebration. Then at the stroke of midnight Shiva is said to manifest as the inner light of purified consciousness. Thus, this climax at night represents our overcoming the dark ignorance and reaching the state of purified spiritual knowledge. Therein we conquer the influence of the mind and senses, exhibited by staying awake all night, and enter the state of steady awareness wherein there is spiritual awakening. If one can follow this process, then he or she can experience the real meaning of Shivaratri.

Holi: Holi is a major festival and celebrates the onset of spring, along with good harvests and the fertility of the land. It is celebrated on the day after the full moon in early March. This festival is known best for the way people throw brightly colored powder and water over each other to celebrate the advent of spring. Then they bathe and cleanse themselves after which they distribute sweets amongst friends and relatives. Vibrant processions accompanied by folk songs and dances are also a characteristic of Holi celebrations. Holi is a very popular festival amongst the youth. Holi also commemorates the burning to death of Holika, the aunt of Prahlada. Huge bonfires are lit on the eve of Holi for this reason. Holi is celebrated with great vigor in the north, but is hardly celebrated in southern India. It is celebrated for the arrival of spring; the victory of Prahlada over his wicked demon father, Hiranyakashipu; and for the death of Hiranyakashipu's sister, Holika, or Holi. The day after Holi is the actual day of colors. On that day, people take colored powder and throw it on each other.

Gaura Purnima: This is the festival that is celebrated by the increasing numbers of the Gaudiya Vaishnava tradition. It is the celebration of the birth of Lord Chaitanya, who was considered an incarnation of God, Lord Krishna. Lord Chaitanya showed by example the highest emotion and sentiment of worship and love for Lord Krishna. He also was the first to start peaceful civil disobedience demonstrations for worshiping the Lord, and the *sankirtana* movement, which is the congregational chanting of the Lord's holy names in the form of the Hare Krishna mantra.

Shri Rama Navami: This festival celebrates the birth of Lord Rama who is an incarnation of Lord Vishnu. This festival is celebrated during the time of March-April, or the ninth lunar day of the bright fortnight. Lord Rama, who became king of Ayodhya, was known for His exemplary qualities. He was popular, brave, kind, just, intelligent, patient, loving, obedient and dutiful. Lord Rama is always worshiped with his consort Sita, brother Lakshmana and devotee Hanuman. The worship of Lord Rama is accompanied by the worship of the Sun god since Rama was considered to have descended from the sun, meaning a part of the Solar dynasty. Rama Navami celebrations include reading the great epic *Ramayana* and staging plays of the Rama Lila, or the pastimes of the life of Lord Rama.

Ugadi and Vishu: These are two festivals that celebrate the New Year in different communities of south India. Ugadi is celebrated in March-April. Vishu is celebrated in mid-April. The word Yugadi means the day of the inauguration of the Yuga or Age. Vishu is celebrated in a big way in Kerala. Families wake up in the morning and make sure they feast their eyes on good things like a picture of God, grains, flowers, fruit and gold. It is believed seeing these first thing in the morning of the New Year will bring them prosperity and wealth throughout the year.

Hanuman Jayanthi: This celebrates the birth of Hanuman, the most famous devotee of Lord Rama. His birthday falls on Chaitra Shukla Purnima—the March-April full moon day. On this holy day devotees worship Sri Hanuman, fast on this day, read the Sri Hanuman Chalisa, and spend the whole day in the Japa of Ram-Nam, chanting the names of Lord Rama. It is said that Hanuman will be highly pleased and will bless you with success in all your undertakings. Celebrations are marked by special *pujas* (rituals of worship) for Hanuman.

Sri Hanuman is worshipped all over India—either alone or together with Sri Rama. Every temple of Sri Rama has the murti or image of Sri Hanuman. Hanuman was the *avatara* of Lord Shiva. He was born of the Wind-God and Anjani Devi. He is also called by the names Pavanasuta, Marutsuta, Mahavira, Bajrangabali and Pavankumar.

Hanuman was the living embodiment of the power of Ram-Nam. He was an ideal selfless worker, a true devotee who worked without personal desires, and an exceptional Brahmachari or celibate. He served Sri Rama with pure love and devotion. He lived only to serve Sri Rama. He was humble, brave and wise. He possessed all the divine virtues. He did what others could not do—crossing the ocean simply by uttering Ram-Nam, burning the demon-king's city of Lanka, and bringing the sanjeevini herb to restore the life of Lakshmana. He brought Sri Rama and Lakshmana from the nether world after killing Ahiravana.

Hanuman possessed devotion, knowledge, spirit of selfless service, power of celibacy, and desirelessness. He never boasted of his bravery and intelligence. He said to Ravana, "I am a humble messenger of Sri Rama. I have come here to serve Sri Rama, to do His work. By the command of Sri Rama, I have come here. I am fearless by the Grace of Sri Rama. I am not afraid of death. I welcome it if it comes while serving Sri Rama."

Sri Rama Himself said to Hanuman, "I am greatly indebted to you, O mighty hero. You did marvelous, superhuman deeds. You do not want anything in return. Sugriva has his kingdom restored to him. Angada has been made the crown prince. Vibhishana has become king of Lanka. But you have not asked for anything at any time. You threw away the precious garland of pearls given to you by Sita. How can I repay My debt of gratitude to you? I will always remain deeply indebted to you. I give you the boon of everlasting life. All will honor and worship you like Myself. Your image will be placed at the door of My temple and you will be worshipped and honored first. Whenever My stories are recited or glories sung, your glory will be sung before Mine. You will be able to do anything, even that which I will not be able to!"

Thus did Sri Rama praise Hanuman when the latter returned to Him after finding Sita in Lanka. Hanuman was not a bit elated. He fell in prostration at the holy feet of Sri Rama.

Sri Rama asked him, "O mighty hero, how did you cross the ocean?" Hanuman humbly replied, "By the power and glory of Thy Name, my Lord." Again Sri Rama asked, "How did you burn Lanka? How did you save yourself?" And Hanuman replied, "By Thy Grace, my Lord." Everyone should try his best to follow the noble example of Hanuman. Glory to Hanuman! Glory to his Lord, Sri Rama!

Guru Purnima: This is a festival with a truly spiritual meaning and relevance. Guru Purnima celebrates the might of one's teacher or guru through respect and reverence. Also known as Vyasa Purnima, the festival is celebrated in July-August on the full moon. It is believed that the great scholar and composer of the Vedic literature, Vyasadeva, who lived in the Dvapara Yuga, was born on this day. Legend also has it that this is when he completed the codification of the four *Vedas*.

This is the day to honor all the gurus who have showed us the path of Dharma and have helped us remove our ignorance.

Onam: This festival marks the day on which the great devotee of Lord Vishnu Emperor Maha Bali, the grandson of Prahlada (the great devotee of Lord Narasimha), received benediction and liberation with the blessings of the Lord, who had assumed the form of Vamanadeva, the dwarf incarnation. Onam is celebrated in August-September, and especially in Kerala. Onam is a ten-day festival marked by women creating beautiful floral patterns in front of their houses, pujas for Lord Vishnu, feasting and boat races.

Raksha Bandan: This celebrates the love of a sister for her brother. *Raksha* means "protection" and *Bandhan* means "tie". On this day, sisters tie a *rakhi*, a colorful bracelet made of silk thread, on the wrist of their brothers to protect them against evil influences. So it is a reminder of brothers to protect their sisters, or the one who ties the Rakhi. Within the Rakhis reside sacred feelings and good wishes. It is celebrated in July-August. Raksha Bandan is celebrated in some parts of India as a festival to honor the sea god Varuna, where coconuts are offered to the sea. Because of its three eyes, the coconut represents the three eyes of Shiva. As a mark of auspiciousness, coconuts are also broken at shrines and temples. This is also the day set apart for Brahmins to change the sacred thread they wear. Priests also tie rachis to the devotees who attend various *pujas* or festivals.

Krishna Janmashtami: This is the celebration of the birth of Lord Krishna. It is celebrated on the eighth day of the dark fortnight in August-September. Temples and homes are beautifully decorated and lit. Notable are the cribs and other decorations depicting stories of Lord Krishna's childhood. In the evening bhajans (devotional songs) are sung which end at midnight, the auspicious moment when Lord Krishna was born. Krishna Janmastami is a festival that is held in the typical pattern of preparation, purification, realization, and then celebration. On the day of the festival, people will fast and spend the day focused on Krishna, meditating and chanting the Hare Krishna mantra and other prayers or songs devoted to Lord Krishna. Often times, there will also be plays and enactments of the birth and pastimes of the Lord. Thus, offering their obeisances, focusing their minds on Lord Krishna, the devotees hold themselves in such single-pointed concentration throughout the day. Then at the stroke of midnight Lord Krishna takes birth, which is celebrated by a midnight *aarati* ceremony. Flowers are showered on the deity of Lord Krishna, or the deities are dressed in new outfits or decorated with numerous flowers on this day. Devotees will often spend time at their local Krishna temple on this day, especially for the midnight celebration.

In this way, after a full day of purification, we realize our own connection with the Lord, who then manifests as the Supreme worshipable object of our purified consciousness. Thus, this climax at night represents our overcoming the darkness of ignorance and reaching the state of purified spiritual knowledge and perception. Therein we overcome the influence of the mind and senses and enter the state of steady awareness wherein there is full spiritual awakening. If one can follow this process, then he or she can experience the real meaning of Krishna Janmastami. Then *prasada* (sacred offered food) is distributed to everyone.

Ganesh Chaturthi: This celebrates the birth of Lord Ganesh, also called Vinayaka, his child form, as he is popularly known in southern India. He is the god of wisdom, prosperity and good luck. He also removes obstacles. Ganesh Chaturthi is celebrated on the fourth day of the lunar month that falls in August-September. Clay figures of the elephant-headed Ganesh are made and after being worshiped for two days, or in some cases ten days, are immersed in water. Ganesh Chaturthi is very popular in the Indian state of Maharasthra.

Navaratri: Navaratri or the nine sacred nights dedicated to the Mother Goddess are celebrated in the month of October-November. Navaratri includes the Sarasvati Puja and the Durga Puja festivals. "Nava" means nine and "ratri" means night. So Navaratri literally means nine nights. It is during these nine nights of festivities that the goddess is worshiped in Her different forms of Durga, Lakshmi and then Sarasvati. Durga is worshiped during the first three nights of the festival because of her destructive aspect. She destroys the *anarthas* or unwanted barriers that hold us back from our true spiritual potential. She reduces the evil tendencies in the mind, which is the meaning of *durgati harini*. Thus, she is worshiped to relieve us of our destructive tendencies of desire, lust, passion, greed, anger, etc. Without removing these obstacles, the spiritual unfoldment cannot take place.

The next step is to apply the positive process of adding the qualities we need. So Lakshmi is worshiped over the next three nights. She gives one the wealth of good qualities, such as love, goodness, compassion, forgiveness, cooperation, nonviolence, devotion, purity, and the like. Virtue is the true wealth, which is given by Lakshmi. This is not merely the wealth of riches and possessions, but the real wealth that can propel us toward the spiritual goal. These positive uplifting qualities replace the bad ones that were removed by Durga.

At this point the seeker can become fit for the philosophical study and contemplation that is required. Then Sarasvati, the goddess of knowledge, is worshiped the remaining three nights. Sarasvati gives one the intelligence, knowledge and wisdom by which spiritual realization is possible. She represents the highest knowledge of the Self. By invoking her blessings, she plays her well-tuned vina of knowledge and insight, which can then tune our mind and intellect for working in harmony with the world and the purpose of our existence. Then our spiritual practice, study, and meditation become effective for producing the victory of rising above the influence of our mind and senses. Then we can perceive our real identity of being spiritual entities and parts of the spiritual dimension, free from illusion.

After having removed our impurities, gained the proper virtues, and then acquired the knowledge of the Self, then the last day is called Vijayadashami, or the day of victory over our minds and the lower dimension after having worshiped the goddess in her three forms. The celebrations of Navaratri are held at night because it represents our overcoming the ignorance of the mode of darkness, the night of *tamoguna*.

Additionally, Navaratri commemorates the day on which the combined powers of the three Goddesses of Durga or Maha-Kali, Maha Lakshmi and Maha Sarasvati put an end to the evil forces represented by the buffalo-headed demon Mahishasura. The ninth day is also the day of the Ayudha Puja in the south. The Ayudha Puja is worship of whatever instruments one may use in one's livelihood. On the proceeding evening, it is traditional to place these instruments on an altar to the Divine. If one can make a conscious effort to see the Divine in the tools and objects one uses each day, it will help one to see one's work as an offering to God. It will also help one to maintain constant remembrance of the Divine. Children traditionally place their study books and writing implements on the altar. Throughout the ninth day, an effort is made to see one's work or studies as imbued with the Divine presence. The tenth day is called Vijaya Dashami. Devotees perform a *puja* to the Goddess Sarasvati to invoke the blessings of Sarasvati on books, writing implements, musical instruments and tools of trade. After the *pujas*, little children are initiated into the learning process.

So the Vedic festivals are performed in these phases of first preparation, then purification, realization, and then celebration. It represents one's progress toward the real goal of life. First the mind must be purified of all unwanted thoughts and habits. Then it must become focused on one's concentration of the Supreme. As the knowledge of our spirituality of the Self and our connection with the Supreme Being becomes revealed, then there is realization. When such realization has been reached and the ego destroyed, then there is celebration. Living life on the basis of spiritual realization means that life is a constant joy and celebration.

Dusshera, also known as Vijaya Dashami, is celebrated on the tenth day of Navaratri. This signifies the victory of Lord Rama over the demon Ravana, which is often observed with special celebrations and the burning of the effigy of Ravana. On that day there is often a huge bonfire in which people burn the effigy of the demon Ravana, which also represents the destruction of the false ego. Thus, it is a festival which shows the process by which humanity can reach the perception of God. It incorporates the means and worship by which one can purify themselves of the ten sins, meaning the sins committed by the ten active senses. It is the process of purification so that one is meant to become free of the dictates of the mind and the temporary world of sense objects, which paves the way for one to enter into the transcendental experience.

What this shows is that all aspects of the Vedic process, whether we are familiar with them or not, are ultimately meant to be a vehicle by which we can transcend the mind, senses, and the temporary material world and enter into the Supreme Reality wherein we can reestablish our lost relationship with the Supreme Being.

Karva Chauth: This is a fast undertaken by married Hindu women who offer prayers seeking the welfare, prosperity and longevity of their husbands. Karva Chauth is celebrated before Deepavali some time in October or November. It is the most important fast observed by the women of North India. A woman keeps such a fast for the welfare of her husband, who becomes her protector after she leaves her parents home. Her husband provides her with food, shelter, clothing, respectability, comfort and happiness. This is a tough fast to observe as it starts before sunrise and ends after worshiping the moon, which usually rises late evening.

Deepavali: Deepavali, or Diwali as it is popularly called, is the festival of lights. It symbolizes the victory of righteousness and the lifting of spiritual darkness. The word Deepavali literally means rows of clay lamps. It is celebrated on the New Moon day of the dark fortnight during October-November. It is also associated with the return to Ayodhya of Lord Rama, His wife Sita and His brother Lakshmana after their fourteen-year sojourn in the forests. The day also marks the coronation of Lord Rama.

The meanings of Diwali, its symbols and rituals, and the reasons for celebration are innumerable. Another is how Lord Krishna tamed and killed the demon King Narakasura. It also commemorates Lord Krishna's victory over the demon Narakasura. It is said that Narakasura, the son of Bhudevi, who ruled the kingdom of Pradyoshapuram, often troubled the devas and disturbed the penance of the sages. Narakasura also had kidnapped and terrorized the gopis (cowherd girls) of Vrindavan. Tired of this harassment, Indra and other devas approached Lord Krishna and pleaded with Him to protect them from the demon Narakasura. But the demon king could only be killed by a woman. So Lord Krishna asked His wife, Satyabhama, the reincarnation of Bhudevi, to be His charioteer in the battle with Narakasura. Lord Krishna waged a fierce battle and killed the demon. When the evil Naraka was finally killed by Bhagwan Krishna and Satyabhaama, he begged pitifully for mercy; thus, upon his entreaties, Bhudevi declared that his death should not be a day of mourning but an occasion to celebrate and rejoice. Since then, Deepavali is celebrated every year with lots of fun and frolic and fireworks. It is also known as Krishna Chaturdashi. It is also celebrated as the day Bhagwan Vishnu married Maha Lakshmi.

Diwali is also associated with the story of the fall of Bali—a demon king who was conquered by Lord Vishnu. Lord Vishnu appeared to the demon king Bali in the form of a dwarf and requested only three steps of land. The evil and egotistic Bali granted the dwarf's meager request of only three feet. Suddenly, Lord Vishnu took on His grand size and placed one foot on the Earth, another on the Heavens and His third on the head of the evil Bali.

In general, Diwali signifies the triumph of good over evil, of righteousness over treachery, of truth over falsehood, and of light over darkness.

Diwali also marks the New Year. For some, the day of Diwali itself is the first day of the New Year, and for others the new year's day is the day following Diwali. But, for everyone this season is one of heralding in the New Year. In the joyous mood of this season, we clean our homes, our offices, our rooms, letting the light of Diwali enter all the corners of our lives. We begin new checkbooks, diaries and calendars. It is a day of "starting fresh".

On this day we clean every room of the house; we dust every corner of the garage, we sweep behind bookshelves, vacuum under beds and empty out cabinets. But, what about our hearts? When was the last time we swept out our hearts? When did we last empty them of all the dirt and garbage that has accumulated throughout our lives?

That is the real cleaning we must do. That is the real meaning of "starting fresh". We must clean out our hearts, ridding them of darkness and bitterness, we must make them clean and sparkling places in which God can live. We must be as thorough with ourselves as we are with our homes. Are there any dark corners in our hearts we have avoided for so long? Are we simply "sweeping all the dirt under the rug?" God sees all and knows all. He knows what is behind every wall of our hearts, what is swept into every corner, and what is hidden under every rug. So this holiday is observed to truly clean out our hearts and rid ourselves of the grudges, pain, and anger that clutter our ability to love freely. We need to empty out every nook and cranny, so that His divine light can shine throughout.

Diwali is celebrated in grand fashion. For some, they have a oil bath early in the morning and wear new clothes. Children love the fireworks associated with Diwali. A lot of sweets are distributed to friends and relatives. And homes are often lit with rows and rows of little clay lamps called *diyas* that light up the dark New Moon night. Businesses begin their new book keeping with Diwali. The trading community celebrates the thirteenth day of the month of Kartika (Oct.-Nov) as Dhanteras or Dhantrayodashi, the first of the five-day festival. The word *Dhan* means wealth, and the day is of great importance for the rich mercantile community of Western India. Their homes and business premises are all decked up in lights to usher in prospering times. The day ends with a Lakshmi *puja* at home. Some temples also conduct large Lakshmi *puja* celebrations.

This is the third and perhaps most important aspect of Diwali: the worship of Maha Lakshmi. Maha Lakshmi is the goddess of wealth and prosperity, bestowing these abundantly upon her devotees. On Diwali we pray to her for prosperity; we ask her to lavish us with her blessings. However, what sort of prosperity are we praying for? All too often, we infer wealth to mean money, possessions, material pleasures. This is NOT the true wealth in life; this is not what makes us prosperous. There is almost no correlation between the amount of money we earn, the number of possessions we buy and our sense of inner bliss and prosperity.

So on Diwali, we must pray to Maha Lakshmi to bestow real prosperity upon us, the prosperity that brings light to our lives and sparkle to our eyes. We should pray for an abundance of faith, not money. We should also pray for success in our spiritual lives, not a promotion at work.

Another point about Maha Lakshmi is that we tend to worship only Her most prominent of aspects—that of bestowing prosperity upon Her devotees. However, She is a multi-faceted goddess, filled with symbols of great importance. As we worship Her, we should look more deeply at Her divine aspects. First, according to the Vedic scriptures, She is the divine partner of Lord Vishnu. In Hindu tradition, there is almost always a pair—a male and a female manifestation of the Divine, and they play interdependent roles. In this way it is said that Maha Lakshmi provides Lord Vishnu with the wealth necessary in order to sustain life. He sustains, but through the wealth She provides.

Therefore, in its highest meaning, Maha Lakshmi provides wealth for sustenance, not for indulgence. Our material wealth and prosperity should only sustain us, giving us that which is necessary to preserve our lives. All surplus should be used for humanitarian causes. She does not give wealth so that we may become fat and lazy; yet, that is what we tend to do with the wealth we receive. Let us remember that Maha Lakshmi's material wealth is meant for sustenance and preservation, not for luxury and decadence.

So on Diwali, decorated and renovated to the hilt, the day begins with a bang of fire crackers with the performance of Lakshmi *puja* in the evenings. To indicate Her long-awaited arrival, small footprints are drawn with rice flour and vermillion powder all over the houses. Entrances are decorated with lovely, colorful motifs of *rangoli* to welcome the Goddess of Wealth and prosperity. Lamps are kept burning all through the nights and women make it a point to purchase some gold or silver, or at least one or two new utensils, as it is considered auspicious and a symbol of prosperity, a manifestation of the goddess Herself. In South India, cows are offered special veneration and are adorned and worshiped as the incarnation of Goddess Lakshmi.

Another interesting story that is related to this day is about the son of King Hima. He was doomed to die of a snakebite on the fourth day of his marriage. The young daughter-in-law of the king, to save her husband, laid out gold ornaments, lots of gold and silver coins in a big heap at the entrance of her husband's boudoir and lighted innumerable lamps all over the place. She kept herself awake the entire night singing songs. When Yama, the Lord of Death, arrived in the guise of a serpent, his eyes were blinded by the dazzle of the brilliant lights, the gold and silver ornaments, and he was unable to enter the Prince's chamber. So he climbed on top of the heap of ornaments and coins and sat there the whole night listening to the melodious songs. In the morning he quietly went away. Thus, the young wife saved her husband. And so the day is also known as Yamadeepdaan and earthen lamps are kept alight throughout the night in the reverential adoration of Yama.

The following day is celebrated as Narka-Chaturdashi or Choti Diwal. Lord Krishna and His wife Satyabhama are said to have returned home victorious after killing demon Narakasura, early in the morning on this day. The Lord was massaged with scented oils and was given a good bath to wash away the filth from His body. Since then, on this day, the custom of taking an oil bath with fragrant *uptan* before sunrise has become a traditional practice in Maharashtra and South India.

The Diwali day is devoted entirely to the propitiation of Goddess Lakshmi, burning lamps, firecrackers, card games and lots of *masti*. On the dark night of Amavasya, businessmen perform Chopda *puja* and open new account books.

The day following Diwali is the day of Govardhana *puja*. According to the *Vishnu Purana*, years ago the people of Gokul near Mathura used to celebrate a festival in honor of Lord Indra and worship him after the end of every monsoon season. However, one year the young Lord Krishna prevented them from offering prayers to Indra and convinced the people to offer the *puja* to Govardhan Hill, since it was an incarnation of the Supreme. This made Lord Indra enraged, who in turn sent a huge flood to submerge Gokul. But Lord Krishna saved Gokul and all the residents by holding aloft Govardhan Hill like an umbrella.

The day is also observed as *annakoot* in temples of Mathura and Nathdwara. This is when the deities are worshiped with innumerable varieties of delicious sweets, which are ceremoniously raised into the form of a mountain of *bhog* (food), which is offered to the Lord and is worshiped as a form of the Govardhan Hill. Afterwards the devotees approach the mountain of food, do *puja* or worship to it and circumambulate it as was originally instructed by Lord Krishna. Later everyone takes portions of it as *prasada,* food that has been offered to the Lord and received as His mercy.

The fifth and final day of the Diwali festival is known as Bhayya-Duj or Bhav-Bij. According to the legend, Lord Yama, the God of Death, visited his sister Yami on this day. She is said to have applied the auspicious *tilok* on his forehead, garlanded him and served him delicious sweets. In return, Yama gave her a special gift as a token of his love and pronounced that anyone who received *tilok* from his sister would never be defeated. And so to this day, brothers never fail to visit their sisters on the final day of Diwali.

With lights everywhere, Diwali symbolizes the dispelling of darkness, ignorance and evil, and a new hope for the future and irrespective of the region, unites the nation in the festivity of prosperity and joy. Diwali is also known for making delicious sweets and giving them as presents.

Gita Jayanthi: This is the celebration of when Lord Krishna spoke the illustrious *Bhagavad-Gita* to His friend Arjuna on the battlefield of Kurukshetra, north of New Delhi. This usually takes place in the early part of the month of December.

10

Other Important Traits Of Vedic Dharma

THE VEDIC PATH HAS A MOST DEVELOPED AND COMPLETE SPIRITUAL PHILOSOPHY

As we can see from the previous description of the Vedic scripture and its philosophy, along with the additional aveneues of Self-discovery and development that it offers, is one of the most extensive spiritual paths you can find anywhere. It covers so many aspects of life, both material and spiritual, that it is more comprehensive than any other philosophy or lifestyle that you can find. So many viewpoints on life, the material manifestation, God, and our spiritual nature have already been thoroughly considered and thought out that there is little, if anything, that the Vedic philosophy has not already dealt with and spoke about. Everything is there, more of which than most people are aware. Because of this it has attracted thinkers and philosophers from all over the world and from all points in time. The West in particular has and still does look to India for the loftiest spiritual knowledge, and for what the churches or synagogues have not delivered. This may include practical spiritual guidance in Self-discovery, an integrated world view, spiritual and emotional fulfillment, and even true mystical or spiritual experiences. The spiritual processes that are explained in the Vedic teachings go far beyond the conventional idea, as presented by most religions, that people should merely have faith and pray to God for forgiveness of their sins in order to be delivered to heaven. Naturally, we all have to be humble before God. That is what is encouraged and developed. This is especially in the loving devotional path, wherein a person can purify his or her consciousness through the spiritual practices that are fully explained in the Vedic teachings, even though this takes time and serious dedication and sincerity.

The point is that the Vedic process does not discourage one from having his or her own spiritual realizations, which are often minimized, neglected or even criticized in other religions that often teach that the church alone is what maintains your connection with God. But in the Vedic system it is taught that we are all spiritual and loving parts of God, and automatically have a relationship with God. Therefore, such experiences are considered a proof that the process is successful at helping one elevate his or her consciousness. One's consciousness resonates at various frequencies, depending on the level of one's thoughts, words and actions, as well as the images and sounds that one absorbs through contact with objects and activities. By learning how to undergo the proper training, one can include the practices that will bring one's consciousness to a level in which one can perceive that which is spiritual. The more spiritual you become, the more you can perceive that which is spiritual. The whole idea is to bring one to perceive his or her spiritual identity and relationship with God. Thus, it must be a scientific process, used under the guidance of a spiritual master for it to be successful. If the process is not complete or if the student is not serious, then of course the results will not be as expected. Yet, if the proper spiritual process is explained correctly, and the student is sincere in his or her efforts, the effects will be there. This is why for thousands of years philosophers and spiritual seekers from around the world have come to India, or have been influenced by the Vedic system: It gives practical results when properly performed.

THE PURPOSE OF HAVING A GURU

In brief, a guru is a spiritual teacher who is knowledgeable in the Vedic scripture and the traditions and can teach it to others. He or she must also be experienced in the spiritual Truths, the goal of the Vedic path, and can thus show the way by example to those who enquire.

The word *guru* means the dispeller of darkness. It also means one who is heavy with knowledge, not only cultivated knowledge acquired through personal training and practice, but also knowledge attained through personal experience and realizations of the spiritual perfection that is discussed in the Vedic scripture and by previous spiritual authorities. Such a qualified guru is one who should be approached with respect and served with humility and honor because such a guru who has seen the Truth can give one knowledge and guidance for attaining the Truth. Such a guru gives the second birth to a person into the spiritual understanding, beyond the common first birth one acquires from parents. Thus, a genuine guru is not someone who tries to control or dominate a person's life but is another means by which a seeker can be guided to attain the highest levels of realization. Such a guru can awaken a disciple to a new world of spiritual reality, a higher dimension. Such an awakening creates an eternal bond between the spiritual master and disciple.

NONVIOLENCE

Nonviolence or *ahimsa* in Vedic culture is an important vow. It means to cause no harm to others in thought, word or deed. In respect to *ahimsa*, nonviolence and non-injury toward all beings is found amongst all Dharmists. It is a means of respecting all life and of recognizing and honoring the Divine in all creatures, not just human beings. No one likes to suffer, and to lead a life in which there is the least amount of suffering caused to others is a prime principle for Hindus. Nonviolence is an aspect of spiritual life. The more we fall from this principle, the less we consider regarding the well-being of others and their connection with God. Thus, nonviolence is the means to live in harmony with all beings.

However, this does not mean that we make no endeavor to defend ourselves from unprovoked and violent attacks that threaten the lives of ourselves or our family and community. Though we never attack others, we must know when to defend ourselves from those who mean to harm us or our community and culture or the Dharma. Otherwise, Hindus are most peaceful and tolerant with everyone and it takes a lot to finally provoke them to any sort of violent action. Thus, most of what has been viewed as Hindu fundamentalism is nothing more than a release of the slow brewing reaction against aggressive and militant conversion tactics of other religions, since India has been viewed as a prime target for that for many years now. Hindus can get along with most anyone, as can be seen by how many religions exist in India; until there is such a lack of reciprocal respect for them and their culture that they feel adjustments need to be made.

COMPASSION IS A PRIME PRINCIPLE OF VEDIC DHARMA

Sometimes people misunderstand that the acceptance of karma, that a person is suffering because of his or her own previous actions, negates the efforts and reasons for assisting in the relief of the suffering of others. A person's actions will certainly produce various results according to their positive or negative qualities. But this does not mean that we should interpret everything that happens to a person in such a way and then become indifferent or callous. Whenever we see the suffering of others we should try to assist them. This is also *ahimsa* or nonviolence. If we can help them but refuse to do so, then that is actually a form of violence. Then, when we may have a need for help, someone may refuse to give us assistance in the same way we treated others.

To understand the suffering of others and have a heartfelt feeling to help them is compassion. It is a means of relating to the struggles that we all must undergo while living in this material world, and recognizing that "there but for the grace of God go I". We all could be in similar situations for one reason or another, and helping others who may need assistance in their suffering provides a special opportunity to recognize the similarity we all share while struggling to exist in this world, and to recognize the presence of God within them. By serving them in their time of despair is also serving God and sharing ourselves in the universal family of God. This is certainly one of the highest expressions of Dharma.

By this principle, Dharmists feel that the mark we make in this world is not one's wealth, fame or power or beauty. It is what we do for others that makes the difference. Sacrificing one's own needs for the benefit of others is unequivocal, and that by serving the parts and parcels of God is a way of serving God.

VEGETARIANISM

Nonviolence is one of the reasons why most devout Hindus are vegetarian. It promotes a greater sensitivity to the Divine in all beings and to the life of all creatures. However, you may see those who are not so serious eating the meat of fish, goat or chicken. At least they do not eat the larger and more important animals. But those who are more sincere about their spiritual life and the progress they make in this life will avoid the consumption of any kind of animals. They know that to satisfy the tongue with meat requires that some living being must be harshly taken and violently killed or slaughtered, and a sensitive Dharmist will not want to participate in such an industry or action. Plus, according to the law of karma, they know that for every action they do, or any action that others are required to do for them, such as the killing or cooking of animals, will later come back to them in an equal amount. So sincere Dharmists will avoid such desires that require animals to be killed or prepared for consumption.

VEDIC DHARMA PROMOTES SEEING GOD IN ALL LIVING BEINGS.

Without a doubt, the Vedic scripture provides descriptions and narrations meant to help one increase his or her awareness of God in all beings. Anyone who studies the essential Vedic texts will soon see a difference in his or her recognition of how God is within everyone, accompanying the *jivatma* (individual soul) as the Paramatma (Supersoul). You will never find anywhere else the information on the Supersoul or descriptions of the individual soul as we find in the Vedic texts.

This information helps us see the Divinity within all living beings and how everyone is a part of the Supreme in spiritual quality. Such an awareness and perception will naturally increase our respect and concern for all living creatures. We will realize that all life is sacred. We will more clearly understand how our love for God will be exhibited by how much we care and cooperate with others.

VEDIC SCRIPTURES DO NOT CONDONE ABORTION

Hindu scriptures also forbid abortion, considering it an extreme act of violence. Various references in the Vedic scriptures actually pray for the protection and well-being of the embryo and bless the parents who can take care of such a child. There are prayers in the *Rig-Veda* to guard a growing embryo. In the codes of Manu, abortion is forbidden. One of the worst acts described in the scriptures is Sis-Hatya, meaning destruction of the defenseless and unborn fetus. There are other verses that describe the punishment of those who put an early end to the child in the womb. Plus, from time immemorial, Hindus consider children as gifts from God. The only time abortion is allowed is when the fetus is known to be defective as per *Susruta Samhita*, the Hindu Ayurveda book.

THE VEDIC PATH VIEWS ALL RELIGIONS AS PORTIONS OF THE ONE TRUTH, AND WAYS OF UNDERSTANDING GOD

There is no discrimination toward other religions in Hinduism. Hinduism views all authentic religions with a potential to raise the consciousness of its followers to a higher level of understanding God, themselves, and humanity. This is merely one of the beautiful aspects of Hinduism or Vedic Dharma; that it provides the greatest latitude of diversity in the ways of understanding God. That is why you can mix Hindus with anyone, and they can peacefully coexist, just as you presently have Hindus, Buddhists, Jains, Sikhs, and others all living together peacefully as can be seen in India. But as soon as you mix those of other religions who are dogmatic in their views, there is trouble. The reason is that there is no room for diversity of thought in such people. They think that in the eyes of God no one else is saved. They think they must "save" everyone by making everyone else just like them. And the way that is done is by converting all others to their own dogmatic beliefs. Thus, they give no credence or understanding toward any religion but their own.

The world could be a peaceful place if it were not for the constant attempt by various groups to control and convert. It is on this account that there have been so many years of bloodshed, slaughter and torture to force others to be of only one religion. Such religions cause themselves not to be united with God, but to stand separated from God for not providing the way to see the spiritual nature and Divinity in all beings. Such religions actually create disharmony between man and God because of forcing their followers to focus on our superficial differences rather than our deeper unity and commonality as beings of one common God.

In this way, Sanatana-dharma is not a religion that stands separate from others. It is not that Hinduism or Vedic culture opposes other spiritual paths. But it represents and provides the means through which anyone can attain the highest spiritual understanding possible. It helps one understand who and what we really are, above and beyond all the superficialities that are often found in the fundamental and materialistic religions. Therefore, once again, anyone, no matter what religion or culture one may be, can still use the Vedic path to increase his or her overall understanding of him or herself, the universe, and God, and awaken our natural spiritual love for one and all.

TRUTH IS ONE, THE NAMES ARE MANY, BUT ALL RELIGIONS ARE NOT THE SAME

Many times there may be those who say that all religions lead to God and are thus all equally valid. Sanatana-dharma does in fact teach that there is one God, one Absolute Truth and source of everything, but all religions do not equally reflect the nature of God. Nor do they all have the same level of knowledge of God. God has various aspects that we should know and understand, but not all religions have this knowledge.

For example, when a person wants to reach the top floor of a tall building, he or she can choose how to get there. One may climb up the stairs, or go up the fire escape, or even scale the exterior of the building like a mountain climber, but the best way is to simply take the elevator. Each way will require certain needs, particular preparations, or knowledge of what to do. The goal may be the same, but the process is different and so are the requirements.

Similarly, religious processes are also different. Some will only give you beliefs to blindly accept, or devotional methods that inspire. Yet some may give more complete avenues that a person can take for deeper levels of personal understanding and experience. The Vedic system is a complete process for understanding and directly perceiving different aspects of the Supreme Reality. Thus, it is most important to choose that process of spiritual development that is most complete and emphasizes personal freedom for individual progress and perception of the Supreme, without the need for relying on elementary dogma.

The spiritual path to God can also be compared to a long highway in which travelers are getting on and off at different points. On a highway from New York to Miami, different people use it to reach different destinations. Some may get on near New York and some get on later, while others may get off long before they reach Miami. Religions are the same way. Some people participate at a high level of consciousness, while others are but beginners. Yet they may get off the highway or the religious path before they have finished their journey. Or certain religions may only have so much knowledge of God to give, so the student has little from which to choose or learn. Thus, they may have to continue the voyage in another life or decide to take a more fulfilling path. In this way, it can become clear that not all religions are the same since they offer different levels of knowledge or methods of practice that culminate in varying stages of understanding. Thus, the goals or results will also vary.

SANATANA-DHARMA HAS SPIRITUAL KNOWLEDGE FOUND NOWHERE ELSE

Sanatana-dharma, Hinduism, contains teachings, knowledge and practices that can be found in few other places or scriptures, and many more found no where else. Therefore, to comprehend the depths of this spiritual understanding, you must dive deep into the Vedic tradition and its sacred texts. For such things as deep meditation, yoga, inner spiritual awakenings, the advanced level of devotion and the direct relations with God, the elaborate descriptions and instructions for such things can be found no where else but in the Vedic texts. They can also be found in the saintly spiritual *acharyas* who have experienced such levels of perception.

For example, there are dictionaries and encyclopedias of all kinds. But some are much bigger and thus more complete than others. So to get the finer details of a topic, you go to the larger encyclopedias. Similarly, there are the abridged and unabridged dictionaries, the latter being complete while the former includes only the most common words. Thus, in the same way, the Vedic system has a whole library of texts to elaborate on any aspect of spiritual understanding and development.

HINDUS ARE NOT INTERESTED IN CONVERTING OTHERS

Hindus do not take it upon themselves to convert others to Hinduism. They never target a certain religion or faith to be subject to their criticism or attempts to be converted to Hinduism. They feel that the focus of any spiritual path should be on God, not on making or accumulating converts like some network marketing scheme that counts profits in terms of the quantity of followers it has. The effort should be in giving high quality spiritual education and, thus, by purity, inspire others to go toward God. Therefore, they have no motive to spread hate or lies or discord amongst any other community or religion. On the other hand, it is seen that Christians often view Hindus as pagans or heathens, meaning, in essence, that they are Godless and doomed to hell, and must accept God in the form of Christianity in order to be "saved". Some Muslims also view Hindus as idolaters or polytheists, and thus damned per the descriptions of the Koran, or so they say. Yet, Hindus are free from any such doctrine or attitude toward Islam or Christianity. Nonetheless, when Hindus begin to react to this constant criticism of their religion by such dogmatists, it is primarily an angry backlash and a defense of their culture rather than an attempt to start friction or trouble with those of other faiths. After all, how long can Hindus continue to be as tolerant as they have been toward those of other religions who are so aggressive in their attempts to make converts and who take advantage of this tolerant attitude? It should be expected that sooner or later Hindus will no longer tolerate this never ending bombardment of propaganda against Hinduism that is used to sway more people toward misunderstanding what Hinduism or Vedic culture is in an effort to make converts.

The desire to convert usually starts with the idea that a person feels their religion is the only one with any validity, or it is "the one true religion" and everyone should join or convert to it. Some even teach that if you are not a member, then you and all other outsiders will go to eternal hell, as if this is the direct punishment from God. This sort of view often leads to great conflict and discord among religions and cultures, all of which is unnecessary. Followers of Sanatana-dharma know that good people can be found in all areas of the world and in all cultures and religions.

However, such Dharmists are always ready to share their spiritual traditions, legends, knowledge and experience with others. This is done to share insights and understanding of life for the benefit that other people can find in them and utilize in their own lives.

If someone becomes interested enough that they want to adopt the Vedic tradition for themselves, Hinduism has always accepted others into its fold and family. Anyone who thinks otherwise does not understand the Vedic process and its openness for all. Thus, they need to be educated that the Vedic tradition has always been universal and accepting of everyone. The idea that you must be born a Hindu to be Hindu, though espoused by some, has never been a part of the real

Vedic process. This concept is all nonsense. Everyone has the freedom to use the tools to grow into higher levels of spiritual development as they see fit. If Hinduism is Santana-dharma, the universal spiritual truths, then how can it not be available to everyone? This is why people all over the world have always looked toward India and its Vedic tradition and Eastern philosophy throughout the ages, and why there is a renaissance of it now.

VEDIC DHARMA HAS NO CONCEPT OF JIHAD, HOLY WARS, CRUSADES, OR MARTYRDOM ON ITS BEHALF

Unlike other religions that tend to be extremists or exceptionally dogmatic in its views, Hinduism, or Vedic culture, has no concepts that relate to being a martyr, as found in Christianity or the Islamic jihad. These are not ideas that make much sense to a follower of the Dharma. Why? Because for Dharmists spiritual life is not about fighting others for the supremacy of one religion over another. Hinduism treats all religions with respect because it has its own sense of security and strength in its approach to God, which is the hallmark of a mature spiritual path. Religion and any spiritual process is to help an individual better understand who he is and what is his or her relation to God, and what is his purpose in the universe. If a person is truly trying to progress in this way, then of what purpose is there in participating in a holy war, or to die becoming a martyr for a cause fighting against another religion? This is not the purpose of any spiritual path. This is why there is not much discussion in the Vedic literature to demean other religions, nor is there any campaign against any so-called "false gods" as you find in the more rigid or dogmatic religions.

The reason for this is not that Hinduism is not interested in "saving" people. The reason is that the Vedic culture allows anyone the freedom to undergo whatever may be necessary for their own spiritual development and particular realizations. The Vedic literature, if studied to its fullest depths, supplies all a person needs in order to understand the highest levels of spiritual Truth. Nonetheless, if a person still has different avenues to investigate in spiritual matters, the Vedic culture allows that person to do so, even if the person may risk undergoing a slow process to the highest levels of spiritual realizations. This is a personal choice for everyone. Therefore, forceful conversions or tyrannical religious rule or competition amongst religions make no sense to the Dharmist. What makes sense is the freedom for each individual to reach an appreciation of everyone being a spiritual being, all going back to God, but at their own pace. Nonetheless, the Vedic spiritual teachers always try to encourage everyone toward the best use of their time and energies in their spiritual pursuits. That is how people are guided in Vedic culture, as opposed to forceful conversions or dogmatic regulations.

Religions that view other spiritual paths as competitors will never understand the Vedic path, which is more open. They will only hold on to their fear that makes them think that only their way is the right way, and all other paths lead to hell, as if they need some reassurance that they are correct. Hinduism does not have such fear of being wrong. Followers of the Vedic path acquire their own spiritual realizations that assure them of their own progress. That is the sign of real spiritual advancement when the change of consciousness is directly perceived. That is the difference between the Vedic path and the more fundamental and fear-based religions that depend mostly on one's blind faith in the process, without experiencing any perceptive results in one's change of awareness and consciousness, or in establishing one's personal relationship with God.

THIS IS WHY THE FOLLOWERS OF THE VEDIC PATH CAN LIVE PEACEFULLY WITH THOSE OF OTHER RELIGIONS

Since Hindus in general, and those with a mature understanding of God as mentioned in the previous point, are more aware of the many different aspects of God, and see the same God in all religions, there is no friction between them and those of other distinct faiths. They can live peacefully with others without the need to feel that everyone else is doomed to hell, or must be converted to be "saved". Hindus recognize the same God though worshiped in many ways. Thus, what is the difficulty? There is no problem. This is true of sincere worshipers of any religion. A sincere and mature Christian can easily get along with a sincere Hindu, who can easily get along with a sincere and mature Muslim, who can get along with a sincere Sikh, and so on.

This is quite different from those fundamental people who label God according to their faith, or who become defensive when apparent differences arise. This is what causes superficial distinctions and designations that grow into religious differences that for a spiritually mature person do not exist. It is only a lack of spiritual and Godly awareness and understanding that keep people pointing fingers at each other and from cooperating and respecting each other. A true religionist can easily recognize another's devotion to God without getting caught up in what may seem to be external differences. It is the essence of spiritual life that matters. That is our focus.

HINDUS OR DHARMISTS PREFER TO SHARE THE VEDIC KNOWLEDGE FREELY

Those who follow Sanatana-dharma are always ready to share the Vedic knowledge with everyone, knowing it is for the benefit of others. However, they do not say it is the only way to God. They also respect other avenues of spiritual understanding. Even the Vedic teachings encourage Dharmists to share the Vedic spiritual understanding. Lord Krishna explains to Arjuna in the *Bhagavad-gita* (18:67-69) that one who shares this knowledge with others is the most dear to God and is assured of reaching God. However, Lord Krishna also explains that one must consider the person's interest and qualifications and not try to share the knowledge with those who are not sincere or inclined to listen. Thus, aggressive proselytizing has no place in Hinduism, but all Dharmists must open this knowledge for the benefit of all who are sincere seekers.

IF HINDUISM DIES OUT

Some Hindus think that if Hinduism fades away, then it must be God's will. But if that were the case, then there never would have been a *Bhagavad-gita*. The Lord would not have given instructions to Arjuna regarding how to do God's will if the Lord did not care. But the Supreme does reciprocate with our sincerity and devotion, but lets mankind follow its own free will. Love is not something that can be forced. You develop love by knowing someone. And you develop God by purifying your consciousness and getting to know God's greatness and characteristics. Then there is the fruition of love which leads to the reciprocation between you and God.

VEDIC DHARMA IS NOT POVERTY BASED

Sometimes people misunderstand the Vedic process and think that it is anti-materialistic, that a devout Hindu should live in poverty. No where does it say that those who follow the path of Sanatana-Dharma should be poverty stricken or without money. The Vedic *shastra* does say that a householder without money is a person in anxiety. Poverty is one of the greatest causes of human suffering. Thus, the Dharma does not support the idea that we should be so anti-materialistic that we become poverty stricken. But the means by which we acquire wealth should be in accord with the Vedic system and executed honestly with generosity and welfare for others. Naturally, Sanatana-Dharma recognizes that gaining wealth is not the most important thing in life. Wealth is often a temporary asset and provides the means for acquiring additional transitory comforts of life. And we do need a certain amount of wealth at least in order to maintain ourselves properly. We should not be in want for the basic necessities of life. However, we also need to know how to live with the essentials of life without more than what is necessary. We also need to depend on God in our spiritual progress, and we can also use our money in the service of God and humanity. By using our money in our service to the Lord, it serves as the basis of purifying and spiritualizing the time we spent in earning the money. So it is not how much wealth we have that makes the difference but how we use it. Furthermore, the Vedic system cautions us that the desire for wealth and materialistic pleasure should be controlled, and not the controller of one's life. True contentment and pleasure comes from understanding our spiritual identity as the Self within.

VEDIC DHARMA TEACHES THAT THE WORLD IS REAL BUT TEMPORARY

Some people may say that the world is an illusion and that we need to be completely detached from it. This is true only to a degree. First, the world and our life in it is real, just as a dream is real until we wake up. The dream we had actually took place, and affected us. Yet, we take it seriously only for as long as we participate in it. When we wake up we no longer take it as reality. We wake up and then get on with our real life. Similarly, this life with our material body and relations is real, but it and everything in this life does not last long. The body we have is always changing, and thus our material identity is not eternal. For that reason it may be called illusory or dream-like. Thus, we need to awaken to our real identity as a spiritual being and regain our spiritual vision to recognize the spiritual nature of all other beings, regardless of their body type or the species in which they reside at the moment. Just as our dreams are very brief in comparison with our regular life, similarly this one lifetime is quite fleeting compared to the eternality of the soul.

THE DHARMA TEACHES THAT DESIRES MERELY NEED TO BE SPIRITUALIZED

Hinduism does not teach that all desires are wrong and that we should be free from every desire. The Dharma does not say that all desires need to be eradicated or stopped. That is actually contrary to our nature. But it does teach that desires need to be spiritualized, or dovetailed in relation to the soul, our real identity. We always have some kind of desires, but they need to be directed in the proper way.

So, it teaches that all desires and actions need to be aimed and fitted into spiritual desires in association with the soul and not the body.

Reaching a state of desirelessness is not really possible. But when all desires and loving propensities are spiritualized so that they are aimed at the needs of the soul and devotion to God, then such desires are no longer considered to be material. The body itself is a great tool for engaging in spiritual advancement. Thus the body needs to be maintained for this kind of service. So it is not unusual to have desires for the maintenance and well-being of our material body. So we work to keep body and soul together in as much as we need it to keep advancing spiritually. But this is not the major goal of life. Spiritual progress is far more important since whatever material advancement we make we must leave behind at the time of death. But whatever spiritual progress we have made stays with the soul lifetime after lifetime.

HINDUS PRACTICE MONOGAMY

Sometimes it is thought that Hindus can marry more than one wife. But Hindus practice monogamy. This is accord with the Vedic premise of purifying one's desires. Thus, a person will not be inclined to look for additional wives or sexual escapades. Even in ancient times it was only the Kshatriya kings who would have more than one wife because with his wealth he could take care of them properly. However, that is a thing of the past. Today in India, it is the Muslims who are allowed to have more than one wife according to their own Sharia or Islamic laws, which is what can create confusion about whether all Indians can marry more than one wife.

HINDU DHARMA DOES NOT TEACH THAT THERE IS A COMPETING EVIL FORCE

God and the Divine energy are to be seen everywhere and within everyone. However, ignorance of this truth is the real cause of evil, discontent, greed and selfish actions. It is a person's intent and result of such selfish intent that is the cause of evil and wrongdoing. When a person seeks to satisfy his or her selfish or evil desires at whatever cost, they may indeed cause or inflict suffering for others.

There is no independent evil force that circulates through the creation making or influencing people to act in wicked ways. But there is the false and immoral aim of life wherein an individual acts in a way that is for his or her own egocentric benefit at whatever the expense may be for others. Even if it means that they kill someone for their own interest. When there are many people who have the same fiendishly selfish outlook, then this becomes a growing vibration and influence, a force that may indeed affect others, either because they become victims of such evil people, or they are influenced to be a part of it.

The way to cure this evil and wickedness is to spread the spiritual vibration and knowledge of God so that everyone can take advantage of it. Then only those who truly dislike God will remain evil. However, where there is light, there can be no darkness. Those who cling to God and the spiritual vibration and knowledge can overcome the influence of evil and wickedness, even if it is that which appears within oneself, or the wickedness that manifests through malevolent beings who may have their own selfish desires to fulfill.

VEDIC DHARMA TEACHES WE SHOULD ACHIEVE GOD'S GRACE

Some people may say that Hinduism does not offer divine forgiveness from God for one's sins, and thus it is easier to accept a religion wherein a person can simply achieve the grace and forgiveness from God by merely accepting certain beliefs. However, it is explained in the Vedic teachings and scriptures that a person is responsible for one's own actions, but the more dedicated and devoted one becomes toward God, the more the Lord will free one from sinful reactions and pave the way for one's deliverance to the spiritual domain. God will provide His causeless mercy and take away the obstacles that distract one from the goal so that the devotee reaches the highest level of the Lord's abode. Lord Krishna explains how His devotee is never lost. (*Bhagavad-gita* 9:31) Lord Krishna also makes it clear that a person should simply surrender to Him and He will deliver him or her from all sinful reactions. Do not fear. (*Bhagavad-gita* 18:66)

Therefore, we see how Sanatana-Dharma also provides the way that even in the most hopeless situation, even for the worst of evil-doers or sinful people, there is a way of reaching spiritual deliverance and purification with the help of God if one is sincere.

THE POSITION OF WOMEN IN A TRULY VEDIC SOCIETY

From a spiritual position, the goal for a woman is the same as that of a man; to attain through spiritual development freedom from the bondage of being in a material body. Therefore, all of the basic moral and spiritual principles of the Dharma are also applicable to her. Thus, she has the freedom to practice as much of the same spiritual path as any man. Nonetheless, it is not overlooked that she is certainly different biologically and psychologically from man. So she has been given certain duties and privileges for her situation. For instance, a woman's ability to be the loving force in the family and in managing the home is definitely recognized. To be a friend and mother is an ideal wife, and in this way compliments the man. In Vedic society men and women are not competitors but are meant to compliment and enhance each others' existence. Nonetheless, women, being biologically weaker than men, were always meant to be protected from the harshness of life or of those who wish to exploit them. This is why it was always recommended that women should always be protected, at first by decent fathers, then by qualified husbands, and then later by respectable sons. Thus, there would always be someone who could look after them.

In the Vedic period women held equal freedom as men. They had equal opportunities in the spiritual path. She was allowed to undergo spiritual initiation by a guru, study the Vedic texts and even to take up monastic life. Only due to foreign invasions from societies that had far less consideration for women were the freedoms that women knew in Vedic India restricted and lost. Now that India is again politically independent are the freedoms that are natural for women and that was known in this land beginning to reappear again in India.

IN ESSENCE, VEDIC DHARMA OPENS THE DOOR TO THE REAL POTENTIALS OF LIFE.

After practicing and living by the principles of the Vedic philosophy, you can bring a perceptive and obvious change in your life, as well as into your own sphere of influence. By beginning to awaken your awareness of your spiritual identity and your relationship with the Supreme, you can easily feel a new level of happiness, peace and contentment. You will have a clearer understanding of who you are, where you have come from, and your purpose in life. You will have a better focus on why we are here and what needs to done while living in this material world. Little things that you may have taken so seriously, that may have bothered you will no longer have the same affect on you. You will see with a clearer view of what really matters in life, and the superficialities that are not important. You will see that there is only one universal religion, and that is Sanatana-dharma, awakening the natural proclivity and needs of the soul, and regaining our real spiritual identity and relationship with God. It is merely a matter of learning how to love and serve God. That is the heart of the Vedic Dharmic path.

11

Who May Be a Hindu or Practice Sanatana-Dharma

Since Sanatana-dharma is a universal process and applicable to everyone, then naturally anyone can practice its principles. Anyone can and should be accepted to participate in the process. Furthermore, anyone who is looking for the ultimate spiritual Truth is already one who is following the path of Sanatana-dharma. So you could say that anyone who is sincerely looking for such Truth with an open mind is already on the spiritual path, at least on some level, and is thus also a Dharmist, a follower of Sanatana-dharma.

The point is that there is one and only one God and one Absolute Truth. The very first of the Vedic books named the *Rig-Veda* proclaims, *Ekam Sat, Viprah Bahudha Vadanti* (There is only one truth, only men describe it in different ways). So a Jew or a Christian or a Muslim who is in search of the Absolute Truth is automatically on the path of Sanatana-dharma. However, if they get stuck with accepting nothing more than their own local traditions, this may hamper their growth in understanding a broader range of the many aspects of the Supreme that are described in other scriptures, such as those of the Vedic literature. So a person's progress depends on how far he or she really wants to go in this lifetime, and how they approach various levels of knowledge to understand the Absolute Truth.

So those who may be accepted as followers of the Vedic tradition generally accept the following: A) The Vedic literature presents knowledge of the Absolute Truth and are the authority on the Vedic tradition; B) There are various ways to realize different aspects of this spiritual Truth; C) God can appear in different forms; D) We are given more than one life on this road of Self-realization; and E) That ultimately we are responsible for accepting the path we take and the progress we make.

To clarify this last statement, even if you accept the path of Christianity and believe that Jesus will save you, Jesus also said that faith alone is not enough. You must show your faith by your works, and your works will show the true state of your desires and consciousness. Otherwise, if by faith alone you go to heaven yet remain full of material or mundane desires for earthly things, do you think Jesus would force you to stay in heaven? No, he would let you go back to earth, to where you heart is, to try and satisfy all those desires because that is your true state of consciousness. So your spiritual advancement is up to you and is revealed by your own level of consciousness, which will take you to the stage of existence in which you are meant to be.

SHARING THE DHARMA

Since we are all eternal spirit souls, part of the Supreme Truth, we are always a part of Sanatana-dharma, or the eternal path to finding the ultimate spiritual Truth. We may call ourselves by whatever religious affiliation we like, but in essence we have a spiritual identity, which the path of Sanatana-dharma assists us in finding.

This spiritual identity is the essence of everyone, making us all similar in our spiritual quality and nature. Your soul is the same as the soul of everyone else. This is our similarity which we all share with every being. Therefore, sincere Hindus will share their philosophy and tradition to provide that assistance and goodwill to others who search for Truth and their higher Selves. It is a way of sharing peace and recognizing that we are all a part of a universal family. For within these bodies of ours exist our real and eternal identity, which is the same within everyone. So everyone can participate and share in the path of Sanatana-dharma.

Sanatana-dharma contains a wealth of spiritual philosophies and practices by which one can enter and experience one's own level of spiritual perception and Self-realization. Some of these may at first seem unusual to a beginner only because other religions do not always teach these systems. They are left out. But the Dharmic path includes many traditions that other religions have forgotten. So these can be helpful for anyone of any religious background. Generally, we find that those who understand the spiritual knowledge of the Vedic system begin to have a deeper understanding of the teachings of other religions as well. This is another aspect of the universality of the spiritual wisdom in the Vedic teachings. Thus, everyone should know this information that is provided within the Vedic path. The point is that the Vedic system provides knowledge for people at whatever level of understanding in which they may be situated.

In this way, the Vedic teachings include spiritual knowledge for the needs of people at all levels. Hinduism does not seek superiority over other religions, but only provides whatever level of knowledge people need. With its library of Vedic literature, it is thus one of the most comprehensive spiritual paths in the world. It only seeks and delivers the highest Truths known to man, and the methods by which a person can realize them for him or herself. Thus, the Vedic path encourages everyone to reawaken their connection with God and realization of the Absolute Truth for themselves, and not necessarily through an institution or organization. The highest Truth is for everyone. Anyone can understand the Vedic path with a little investigation.

However, there have been times when I have heard of individuals or even groups of people, after spending much time in research and discussion, who have decided to become Hindus or devotees. Thereafter, they have come to a Hindu temple and asked to be accepted into the Hindu fold. Then the priest, depending on what kind of temple it is, might say something like one does not need to become a Hindu, but simply go on as you are and become perfect in that way, whether it may be Christian, Muslim, or something else. Thus, the people are turned away with little else to do but continue on a path that they may find to be no longer suitable for them, or that does not fulfill their inner spiritual longings or quest for deeper spiritual knowledge and realizations. If a person finds that they are ready to move forward to a deeper spiritual path, then to deny them that right is not proper, especially by one who may be considered to be a Hindu priest. He should allow them full facility to scan the depths of Vedic spiritual knowledge and to participate to the fullest that they may want in order to increase their devotion and connection with God through this means of expression. So, this confusion must be rectified.

The goal of the Vedic system is to provide the means that anyone can use to raise their consciousness and know God. This point has been advocated by such prominent teachers as Swami A. C. Bhaktivedanta Prabhupada, Swami Vivekananda, Ramana Maharshi, and many others. In this way, for many years the Vedic path has been assimilating those who are willing to adopt the basic principles of Sanatana-dharma, even if they are foreigners. The Vedic temples and the Hindu community must open their doors to those who are seekers of higher Truths, which are abundantly found in Sanatana-dharma. The doors cannot be kept closed for such people who may be looking for the benefits of such spiritual knowledge. Thus, sharing Vedic Dharma with all others who are interested for their benefit has been encouraged by spiritual authorities and should be considered a Dharmic principle.

BECOMING A DHARMIST OR DEVOTEE IS EASY

Does one have to convert to be a Hindu, or undergo a change of names or outward identity? No. If one likes the Vedic philosophy, then one can easily adopt any portion that they find helpful for them. However, if one prefers to use the Vedic culture as a strong basis of one's life and feels devotion toward the path, then there is also nothing wrong with undergoing the formality of a Shuddhi or purification ritual to formally become a Hindu or Sanatana-Dharmist. However, once we adopt the Vedic tradition, this does not mean that we lose our freedom or whatever other roots we had, nor do we need to disrespect whatever other religious tradition we had previously followed. It does not work like that, but this is up to one's own preference. In this way, Sanatana-dharma is inclusive. It allows anyone to find and follow Truth wherever one finds it. Thus, one needs to merely live in a Dharmic lifestyle as outlined by the Vedic principles, which is meant to accelerate one's spiritual advancement and purity in consciousness.

I have often heard that there is a little confusion about what a person should do when they decide to partake of the Hindu religion or become a devotee. This is especially the case if one is a westerner or born as a non-Hindu. Even when the priests at Hindu temples are approached by someone who wants to become a Hindu who is not Indian born, they often do not know what to do. Sometimes it is thought that one must first undergo some kind of formality to make their dedication to their new spiritual path official, like partaking in a ritual or name change or something. A person can do that if one wishes but to merely accept the Vedic path does not require that. To be a Hindu does not require any formality. All it takes is to understand and begin following the Vedic principles to the degree to which one can do so. Of course, one may take initiation from a spiritual master later on, which then may require a formal ritual, depending on the decisions of the guru in this regard. But that is usually a later development.

Sometimes people say that to be a Hindu one has to be born a Hindu. But this is completely wrong. Nowhere in the Vedic *shastra* does it say such a thing. Also, merely being born in a Hindu family does not mean that such a person will have a natural proclivity toward spiritual truth. They may or may not be interested, depending on their level of awareness. Plus, a person may be born in a Hindu family and convert to some other religion. Besides, if Sanatana-Dharma is based on Universal Truth, and what is universal includes everyone, then how can anyone not be included within Sanatana-Dharma if they choose to do so? Thus, the only requirement for being a part of the Vedic path is to accept the basic principles and codes of conduct of Vedic Dharma, as has been outlined in this book. It does not depend on the circumstances of one's birth, such as family, ethnic group, cultural heritage or geographical location. Birth is not more important than one's conduct and character.

The point is that if we are all spirit souls, then the bodily consideration plays no part in the importance to regain the understanding and realization of our spiritual identity. In fact, the more spiritual we become, we find that the less emphasis there will be on the body. Thus, everyone should find and participate in that path which allows one to best rise above bodily identifications. Thus, it does not take a special ceremony or conversion rite to allow anyone to become a participant of the Vedic path. We are all spiritual beings. The human body is merely a machine and covering of the soul. That is the essence of the Vedic teachings. So how does the machine determine which spiritual path we can or cannot take? And as spiritual beings, we have a right and obligation to reach the highest spiritual knowledge and attain the clearest spiritual realizations that we can. If we find that the Vedic teachings can do this and assist us in living the path that allows us to enter such a lofty understanding, then it does not take any special ritual for us to begin the path. All we need to do is to start.

In this way, Sanatana-dharma, which essentially means the eternal nature of the spiritual being or soul, is the path for us to attain that realization of our true spiritual identity and the means to awaken to our real spiritual nature. As spiritual beings, everyone has the right to engage in that process. All one needs to do is add the various Vedic principles to one's life.

Therefore, it should be clear that as we are all spiritual beings in a material body, what difference does the body make in allowing one to participate in the Vedic spiritual process? Anyone can become a member of the Vedic community, and if one temple does not recognize him or her due to their own limited conceptions of who can be a Hindu, then there are other temples wherein a person can be welcomed and participate to a fuller extent. So any interested person should find those temples. Otherwise, all that is required for one to be a Hindu or devotee is faith and practice. And as one progresses, he or she may take up particular forms of yoga, adopt a vegetarian diet, learn to chant certain uplifting prayers or mantras at home, and rise early to do meditation or worship. One may also make an altar at home so that his or her dwelling becomes a temple or has a shrine room. And, of course, one is always encouraged to read the various spiritual texts at home to increase his or her own understanding and awareness, and to focus one's consciousness on the higher purpose of life.

If one wants to make a significant event in which one marks his or her new dedication to the Vedic path, there are different ways in which to do that. There are simple ways, and those that are more formal. For example, a person may simply go to the temple and stand in front of the deity and say, "My dear Lord, from this day on I am Yours. Now kindly accept and guide me." One may even do that in front of a photo or picture of the deity. Then one's progress or entrance into the Vedic process is between you and God, which is the real case anyway. The Vedic texts say that once you surrender yourself to the Lord in this way, you now become His ward. He will give you protection and guidance to the degree to which you depend on Him and wish to serve Him and rekindle your relationship.

If, however, a person wants to increase his or her participation and join an ashrama, then of course there may be particular rules or regulations that one must follow, or adopt certain forms of dress to enhance one's spiritual consciousness, depending on the spiritual discipline involved. But this is not the case if one simply wants to live at home, practice the Vedic principles and be part of the temple congregation. At home, especially if one has a job or career, or a family, a person may accept those practices that best fit into one's life. But then as you progress, you can adjust your life accordingly to make it increasingly spiritual and to accommodate more of the practices that are suggested for your advancement.

There are, however, certain ceremonies one may undergo as a formality, such as the Shuddhi purification rite or the *namakarana samskara* in which one gets a Vedic name, or the initiation by a guru into a particular *sampradaya* or lineage in spiritual practice. Yet, merely adopting the Vedic customs is enough to be considered a follower of the Vedic Dharma. It is the heartfelt faith that is the most important, which is purely an individual prerogative. If someone chooses to be a follower of Vedic Dharma and acknowledges the basic tenets of the Hindu faith, then he is one. He or she does not need to first undergo the formalities to receive the higher spiritual insights in the Vedic practices, such as yoga, meditation, or the study of the Vedic teachings.

In any case, whether living at home or in a temple ashrama, if a person does later find that they would like to continue one's involvement in the Vedic path or join a particular *sampradaya*, or are attracted to take initiation from a particular spiritual master or guru, then they may undergo the initiatory process. Then, depending on the standards of the guru, there may be an initiation ceremony. This is often when a person will get a spiritual name to indicate their new life or spiritual beginning. If one lives in an ashrama at the time, such an initiation ceremony may or may not include that one shave his head, or adopt a certain standard of clothes, and begin chanting a certain mantra in accordance with the process of that level of initiation.

In fact, in taking to the Vedic spiritual life, finding a proper teacher is one of the few injunctions that are presented in the Vedic texts, such as the *Bhagavad-gita*. Therein it relates that in order to make further progress on the path of spiritual realization, one should take instruction from a proper spiritual master. Lord Krishna says: "Just try to learn the truth by approaching a spiritual master. Inquire from him submissively and render service unto him. The self-realized soul can impart knowledge unto you because he has seen the truth." (*Bg.*4.34)

You will notice that the verse does not say that the guru should only accept a person from a certain nationality, religion or culture. The person needs only to be sincere and respectful. The disciple also needs to make sure the guru is genuine and able to deliver the spiritual message of the Lord properly. Thus, it is a reciprocal relationship between the guru and the disciple. But anyone can approach a master for understanding the higher spiritual truths. Once the relationship between the guru and disciple is firmly established, then the guru may then give the initiation ceremony to the disciple for continued spiritual progress.

THE BASICS OF A DAILY ROUTINE

It is accepted that an ideal routine to practice while on the Vedic path is to rise early before sunrise. At that time one may first offer obeisances to your favorite deity. Then take a daily bath or shower and engage in personal worship and prayers to the deity of your choice. Perform meditation, prayers, recitation of sacred texts, sing devotional songs, and engage in *japa*, the chanting of the holy names of God in the form of mantra meditation. This is where a family shrine or temple room becomes most beneficial, unless of course one lives near a temple that can easily be visited at this time. One may also offer food as breakfast to the household deity and then take that food as your *prasada* breakfast, honoring or eating what had been offered to your deity as the remnants of the Lord. Then after one has performed their morning *sadhana* (spiritual practice) one may then engage in the normal activities of one's profession, such as go off to one's career or occupation. For a housewife or mother, she may spend her day engaged in household activities and the care of the children. A career should also be of the type wherein one does not act contrary to the principles of Dharma. Of course, if one is living in an ashrama or temple, then going off to work is generally not a consideration, but one stays in continued spiritual service within the environment of the ashrama or temple.

In the evening, after returning from one's job, it is also beneficial to spend some time in reading sacred books, offering some prayers of appreciation to the deity, or doing some additional meditation to recover from the day's activities and put them behind you, and to again focus on the spiritual goals of life.

Additionally, one should go to the local Vedic or Hindu temple on a regular basis, like once a week or more. It is also a nice idea to engage in service at the temple or to assist in its programs. At least one should also observe the important holidays and Dharmic festivals with reverence and faith at a nearby temple. Going on pilgrimage when it is possible to some of the holy places in India is also a plus for one's spiritual development.

Conclusion
The Future

As a result of this growing search for Truth, humanity is increasingly approaching and exploring the older traditions again to view the deeper levels of spiritual understanding that they contain. As people of the world gain interest in the mystical, the spiritual, yogic and deeper sides of all religions, the movements that recognize these various teachings will grow. This is already happening with the new interest in such topics as yoga, Eastern philosophy, Buddhism, Native American traditions, Pagan practices, and other indigenous cultures. The Sanskrit jargon such as yoga, karma, mantras, chakras, and gurus are now commonplace and are utilized as the basis of new insights. This is a sign that the universality that is inherent in the Vedic traditions are especially becoming more apparent, as its name, Sanatana-dharma, the eternal tradition of Truth, makes so clear.

Sanatana-dharma remains the oldest and most dynamic of all the world's religions and living indigenous cultures. It also remains in the forefront of those paths that emphasize experiential spirituality and shows great freedom in its approach to personal spiritual life. Thus, Vedic culture is experiencing a revival and displays a growing influence all over the world. This is only one of the reasons why it has survived for many thousands of years, in spite of the pressure it and its followers have undergone in the attempt to end its existence by those religions that are more dogmatic and belief oriented.

The more people understand the openness of Sanatana-dharma, the more likely there could be an end to religious war and misunderstandings. In fact, the more likely religion as we know it will give way for the real and personal search for God and Truth, which are principles encapsulated by the Vedic tradition. Religion must be founded on eternal Truth and not merely on humanity's ever-changing opinion and conventions. Otherwise, it is not wholesome or progressive but is artificial and dictatorial and will lead to more religious conflicts in the battle over who is right and who is wrong, and the ways to eliminate all who believe differently than the dominating system. This does little but to preserve the chaos that we see so much of in society today. And the cure from this is what Sanatana-dharma can provide if we investigate it seriously.

◆   ◆   ◆

For a much more thorough explanation of the various aspects of Vedic culture and its spiritual path, see the books by Stephen Knapp, such as *The Secret Teachings of the Vedas* and *The Heart of Hinduism: The Eastern Path to Freedom, Empowerment and Illumination*, which gives a complete course in understanding the Vedic philosophy and how to practice it.

Glossary

Acarya—the spiritual master who sets the proper standard by his own example.

Advaita—nondual, meaning that the Absolute Truth is one, and that there is no individuality between the Supreme Being and the individual souls which merge into oneness, the Brahman, when released from material existence. The philosophy taught by Sankaracharya.

Ahimsa—nonviolence.

Akarma—actions which cause no *karmic* reactions.

Akasha—the ether, or etheric plane; a subtle material element in which sound travels.

Amrita—the nectar of immortality derived from churning the ocean of milk.

Ananda—spiritual bliss.

Ananta—unlimited.

Arati—the ceremony of worship when incense and ghee lamps are offered to the Deities.

Arca-vigraha—the worshipable Deity form of the Lord made of stone, wood, etc.

Aryan—a noble person, one who is on the Vedic path of spiritual advancement.

Asana—postures for meditation, or exercises for developing the body into a fit instrument for spiritual advancement.

Asat—that which is temporary.

Ashrama—one of the four orders of spiritual life, such as *brahmacari* (celibate student), *grihastha* (married householder), *vanaprastha* (retired stage), and *sannyasa* (renunciate); or the abode of a spiritual teacher or *sadhu*.

Astanga-yoga—the eightfold path of mystic yoga.

Atma—the self or soul. Sometimes means the body, mind, and senses.

Avatara—an incarnation of the Lord who descends from the spiritual world.

Aum—om or *pranava*

Ayurveda—the original wholistic form of medicine as described in the Vedic literature.

Badrinatha—one of the holy places of pilgrimage in the Himalayas, and home of the Deity Sri Badrinatha along with many sages and hermits.

Bhagavan—one who possesses all opulences, God.

Bhajan—song of worship.

Bhakta—a devotee of the Lord who is engaged in *bhakti-yoga*.

Bhakti—love and devotion for God.

Bhakti-yoga—the path of offering pure devotional service to the Supreme.

Bhava—preliminary stage of love of God.

Brahma—the demigod of creation who was born from Lord Vishnu, the first created living being and the engineer of the secondary stage of creation of the universe when all the living entities were manifested.

Brahmacari—a celebate student, usually five to twenty-five years of age, who is trained by the spiritual master. One of the four divisions or *ashramas* of spiritual life.

Brahmajjyoti—the great white light or effulgence which emanates from the body of the Lord.

Brahman—the spiritual energy; the all-pervading impersonal aspect of the Lord; or the Supreme Lord Himself.

Brahmana or brahmin—one of the four orders of society; the intellectual class of men who have been trained in the knowledge of the *Vedas* and initiated by a spiritual master.

Brahmana—the supplemental books of the four primary *Vedas*.

Caitanya Mahaprabhu—the most recent incarnation of the Lord who appeared in the 15th century in Bengal and who originally started the *sankirtana* movement, based on congregational chanting of the holy names.

Caranamrita—the water that has been used to bathe the Deity and is offered in small spoonfuls to visitors in the temple.

Causal Ocean or Karana Ocean—is the corner of the spiritual sky where Maha-Vishnu lies down to create the material manifestation.

Chakra—a wheel, disk, or psychic energy center situated along the spinal column in the subtle body of the physical shell.

Chit—eternal knowledge.

Darshan—the devotional act of seeing and being seen by the Deity in the temple.

Deity—the *arca-vigraha*, or worshipful form of the Supreme in the temple, or deity as the worshipful image of the demigod.

Devas—demigods or heavenly beings from higher levels of material existence, or a godly person.

Dharma—the essential nature or duty of the living being.

Dualism—as related in this book, it refers to the Supreme as both an impersonal force (Brahman) as well as the Supreme Person.

Durga—the form of Parvati, Shiva's wife, as a warrior goddess known by many names according to her deeds.

Dvapara-yuga—the third age which lasts 864,000 years.

Dwaita—dualism, the principle that the Absolute Truth consists of the infinite Supreme Being along with the infinitesimal, individual souls.

Gandharvas—the celestial angel-like beings who have beautiful forms and voices, and are expert in dance and music, capable of becoming invisible and can help souls on the earthly plane.

Ganesh—a son of Shiva, said to destroy obstacles (as Vinayaka) and offer good luck to those who petition him. It is generally accepted that the way Ganesh got the head of an elephant is that one time Parvati asked him to guard her residence. When Shiva wanted to enter, Ganesh stopped him, which made Shiva very angry. Not recognizing Ganesh, Shiva chopped off his head, which was then destroyed by one of Shiva's goblin associates. Parvati was so upset when she learned what had happened, Shiva, not being able to find Ganesh's original head, took the head of the first creature he saw, which was an elephant, and put it on the body of Ganesh and brought him back to life. The large mouse carrier of Ganesh symbolizes Ganesh's ability to destroy all obstacles, as rodents can gradually gnaw their way through most anything.

Ganges—the sacred and spiritual river which, according to the *Vedas*, runs throughout the universe, a portion of which is seen in India. The reason the river is considered holy is that it is said to be a drop of the Karana Ocean outside of the universe that leaked in when Lord Vishnu, in His incarnation as Vamanadeva, kicked a small hole in the universal shell with His toe. Thus, the water is spiritual as well as being purified by the touch of Lord Vishnu.

Gangotri—the source of the Ganges River in the Himalayas.

Garbhodakasayi Vishnu—the expansion of Lord Vishnu who enters into each universe.

Gaudiya *sampradaya*—the school of Vaishnavism founded by Sri Caitanya.

Gayatri—the spiritual vibration or *mantra* from which the other *Vedas* were expanded and which is chanted by those who are initiated as *brahmanas* and given the spiritual understanding of Vedic philosophy.

Goloka Vrindavana—the name of Lord Krishna's spiritual planet.

Gosvami—one who is master of the senses.

Govinda—a name of Krishna which means one who gives pleasure to the cows and senses.

Grihastha—the householder order of life. One of the four *ashramas* in spiritual life.

Gunas—the modes of material nature of which there is *sattva* (goodness), *rajas* (passion), and *tamas* (ignorance).

Guru—a spiritual master.

Hare—the Lord's pleasure potency, Radharani, who is approached for accessibility to the Lord.

Hari—a name of Krishna as the one who takes away one's obstacles on the spiritual path.

Haribol—a word that means to chant the name of the Lord, Hari.

Harinam—refers to the name of the Lord, Hari.

Hatha-yoga—a part of the yoga system which stresses various sitting postures and exercises.

Impersonalism—the view that God has no personality or form, but is only an impersonal force (Brahman) which the individual souls merge back into when released from material existence.

Impersonalist—those who believe God has no personality or form.

Incarnation—the taking on of a body or form.

ISKCON—International Society for Krishna Consciousness.

Jagannatha——Krishna as Lord of the Universe, especially as worshipped in Jagannatha Puri.

Jai or *Jaya*—a term meaning victory, all glories.

Japa—the chanting one performs, usually softly, for one's own meditation.

Japa-mala—the string of beads one uses for chanting.

Jiva—the individual soul or living being.

Jivanmukta—a liberated soul, though still in the material body and universe.

Jiva-shakti—the living force.

Jnana—knowledge which may be material or spiritual.

Jnana-kanda—the portion of the *Vedas* which stresses empirical speculation for understanding truth.

Jnana-yoga—the process of linking with the Supreme through empirical knowledge and mental speculation.

Kali—the demigoddess who is the fierce form of the wife of Lord Shiva. The word *kali* comes from *kala*, the Sanskrit word for time: the power that dissolves or destroys everything.

Kali-yuga—the fourth and present age, the age of quarrel and confusion, which lasts 432,000 years and began 5,000 years ago.

Kalki—future incarnation of Lord Vishnu who appears at the end of Kali-yuga.

Kalpa—a day in the life of Lord Brahma which lasts a thousand cycles of the four *yugas*.

Kama—lust or inordinate desire.

Karanodakasayi Vishnu (Maha-Vishnu)—the expansion of Lord Krishna who created all the material universes.

Karma—material actions performed in regard to developing one's position or for future results which produce *karmic* reactions. It is also the reactions one endures from such fruitive activities.

Karma-kanda—the portion of the *Vedas* which primarily deals with recommended fruitive activities for various results.

Karma-yoga—system of yoga for using one's activities for spiritual advancement.

Karmi—the fruitive worker, one who accumulates more *karma*.

Kirtana—chanting or singing the glories of the Lord.

Krishna—the name of the original Supreme Personality of Godhead which means the most attractive and greatest pleasure. He is the source of all other incarnations, such as Vishnu, Rama, Narasimha, Narayana, Buddha, Parashurama, Vamanadeva, Kalki at the end of Kali-yuga, etc.

Krishnaloka—the spiritual planet where Lord Krishna resides.

Kshatriya—the second class of *varna* of society, or occupation of administrative or protective service, such as warrior or military personel.

Ksirodakasayi Vishnu—the Supersoul expansion of the Lord who enters into each atom and the heart of each individual.

Kuruksetra—the place of battle 5,000 years ago between the Pandavas and the Kauravas ninety miles north of New Delhi, where Krishna spoke the *Bhagavad-gita*.

Kurma—incarnation of Vishnu as a tortoise.

Lakshmi—the goddess of fortune and wife of Lord Vishnu.

Lila—pastimes.

Lilavataras—the many incarnations of God who appear to display various spiritual pastimes to attract the conditioned souls in the material world.

Linga—the formless symbol of Lord Shiva, often represents universal space.

Mahabharata—the great epic of the Pandavas, which includes the *Bhagavad-gita*, by Vyasadeva.

Maha-mantra—the best *mantra* for self-realization in this age, called the Hare Krishna *mantra*.

Mahatma—a great soul or devotee.

Mahat-tattva—the total material energy.

Maha-Vishnu or Karanodakasayi Vishnu—the Vishnu expansion of Lord Krishna from whom all the material universes emanate.

Mandir—a temple.

Mantra—a sound vibration which prepares the mind for spiritual realization and delivers the mind from material inclinations. In some cases a *mantra* is chanted for specific material benefits.

Maya—illusion, or anything that appears to not be connected with the eternal Absolute Truth.

Mayavadi—the impersonalist or voidist who believes that the Supreme has no form.

Moksha—liberation from material existence.

Mukunda—Krishna as the giver of spiritual liberation.

Narasimha—Lord Vishnu's incarnation as the half-man half-lion who killed the demon Hiranyakashipu.

Narayana—the four-handed form of the Supreme Lord.

Nataraja—King of Dance, usually referring to Shiva, but also Krishna.

Nirguna—without material qualities.

Nirvana—the state of no material miseries, usually the goal of the Buddhists or voidists.

Om or *Omkara*—*pranava*, the transcendental *om mantra*, generally referring to the attributeless or impersonal aspects of the Absolute.

Paramahamsa—the highest level of self-realized devotees of the Lord.

Paramatma—the Supersoul, or localized expansion of the Lord.

Parampara—the system of disciplic succession through which transcendental knowledge descends.

Parashurama—incarnation of Vishnu with an axe who cleansed the world of the deviant *kshatriya* warriors.

Patanjali—the authority on the *astanga-yoga* system.

Prana—the life air or cosmic energy.

Pranayama—control of the breathing process as in *astanga* or *raja-yoga*.

Prasada—food or other articles that have been offered to the Deity in the temple and then distributed amongst people as the blessings or mercy of the Deity.

Prema—matured love for Krishna.

Puja—the worship offered to the Deity.

Pujari—the priest who performs worship, *puja*, to the Deity.

Radha—Krishna's favorite devotee and the personification of His bliss potency.

Raja-yoga—the eightfold yoga system.

Rajo-guna—the material mode of passion.

Ramachandra—an incarnation of Krishna as He appeared as the greatest of kings.

Ramayana—the great epic of the incarnation of Lord Ramachandra.

Rishi—saintly person who knows the Vedic knowledge.

Sacrifice—to engage in an austerity of some kind for a higher, spiritual purpose.

Shabda-brahma—the original spiritual vibration or energy of which the *Vedas* are composed.

Sat-chit-ananda-vigraha—the transcendental form of the Lord or of the living entity which is eternal, full of knowledge and bliss.

Sadhana—a specific practice or discipline for attaining God realization.

Sadhu—Indian holy man or devotee.

Saguna Brahman—the aspect of the Absolute with form and qualities.

Samadhi—trance, the perfection of being absorbed in the Absolute.

Samsara—rounds of life; cycles of birth and death; reincarnation.

Sanatana-dharma—the eternal nature of the living being, to love and render service to the supreme lovable object, the Lord.

Sankhya—analytical understanding of material nature, the body, and the soul.

Sankirtana-yajna—the prescribed sacrifice for this age: congregational chanting of the holy names of God.

Sannyasa—the renounced order of life, the highest of the four *ashramas* on the spiritual path.

Sarasvati—the goddess of knowledge and intelligence.

Sattva-guna—the material mode of goodness.

Satya-yuga—the first of the four ages which lasts 1,728,000 years.

Shaivites—worshipers of Lord Shiva.

Shastra—the authentic revealed scripture.

Shiva—the benevolent one, the demigod who is in charge of the material mode of ignorance and the destruction of the universe. Part of the triad of Brahma, Vishnu, and Shiva who continually create, maintain, and destroy the universe. He is known as Rudra when displaying his destructive aspect.

Smaranam—remembering the Lord.

Smriti—the traditional Vedic knowledge "that is remembered" from what was directly heard by or revealed to the *rishis*.

Sravanam—hearing about the Lord.

Sri, Sridevi—Lakshmi, the goddess who embodies beauty and prosperity, wife of Lord Vishnu.

Srimad-Bhagavatam—the most ripened fruit of the tree of Vedic knowledge compiled by Vyasadeva.

Sruti—scriptures that were received directly from God and transmitted orally by *brahmanas* or *rishis* down through succeeding generations. Traditionally, it is considered the four primary *Vedas*.

Sudra—the working class of society, the fourth of the *varnas*.

Surya—Sun or solar deity.

Svami—one who can control his mind and senses.

Tamo-guna—the material mode of ignorance.

Tapasya—voluntary austerity for spiritual advancement.

Tilok—the clay markings that signify a person's body as a temple, and the sect or school of thought of the person.

Tirtha—a holy place of pilgrimage.

Treta-yuga—the second of the four ages which lasts 1,296,000 years.

Tulasi—the small tree that grows where worship to Krishna is found. It is called the embodiment of devotion, and the incarnation of Vrinda-devi.

Upanishads—the portions of the *Vedas* which primarily explain philosophically the Absolute Truth. It is knowledge of Brahman which releases one from the world and allows one to attain self-realization when received from a qualified teacher. Except for the *Isa Upanishad*, which is the 40th chapter of the *Vajasaneyi Samhita* of the *Sukla* (*White*) *Yajur-veda*, the *Upanishads* are connected to the four primary *Vedas*, generally found in the *Brahmanas*.

Vaikunthas—the planets located in the spiritual sky.

Vaishnava—a worshiper of the Supreme Lord Vishnu or Krishna and His expansions or incarnations.

Vaisya—the third class of society engaged in business or farming.

Vamana—dwarf incarnation of Vishnu who covered the universe in three steps.

Vanaprastha—the third of the four *ashramas* of spiritual life in which one retires from family life in preparation for the renounced order.

Varaha—Lord Vishnu's boar incarnation.

Varna—sometimes referred to as caste, a division of society, such as *brahmana* (a priestly intellectual), a *kshatriya* (ruler or manager), *vaisya* (a merchant, banker, or farmer), and *sudra* (common laborer).

Varnashrama—the system of four divisions of society and four orders of spiritual life.

Vasudeva—Krishna.

Vedanta-sutras—the philosophical conclusion of the four *Vedas*.

Vedas—generally means the four primary *samhitas; Rig, Yajur, Sama, Atharva*.

Venktateshvara—Vishnu as Lord of the Venkata Hills, worshiped in Tirumala.

Vidya—knowledge.

Vikarma—sinful activities performed without scriptural authority and which produce sinful reactions.

Virajanadi or Viraja River—the space that separates the material creation from the spiritual sky.

Vishnu—the expansion of Lord Krishna who enters into the material energy to create and maintain the cosmic world.

Vrindavana—the place where Lord Krishna displayed His village pastimes 5,000 years ago, and is considered to be part of the spiritual abode.

Vyasadeva—the incarnation of God who appeared as the greatest philosopher who compiled the main portions of the vedic literature into written form.

Yajna—a ritual or austerity that is done as a sacrifice for spiritual merit, or ritual worship of a demigod for good *karmic* reactions.

Yamaraja—the demigod and lord of death who directs the living entities to various punishments according to their activities.

Yamuna—goddess personification of the Yamuna River.

Yantra—a machine, instrument, or mystical diagram used in ritual worship.

Yoga—linking up with the Absolute.

Yoga-*siddhi*—mystic perfection.

Yuga-avataras—the incarnations of God who appear in each of the four *yugas* to explain the authorized system of self-realization in that age.

Index

About Stephen Knapp

Stephen Knapp grew up in a Christian family, during which time he seriously studied the Bible to understand its teachings. In his late teenage years, however, he sought answers to questions not easily explained in Christian theology. So he began to search through other religions and philosophies from around the world and started to find the answers for which he was looking. He also studied a variety of occult sciences, ancient mythology, mysticism, yoga, and the spiritual teachings of the East. After his first reading of the *Bhagavad-gita*, he felt he had found the last piece of the puzzle he had been putting together through all of his research. Therefore, he continued to study all of the major Vedic texts of India to gain a better understanding of the Vedic science.

It is known amongst all Eastern mystics that anyone, regardless of qualifications, academic or otherwise, who does not engage in the spiritual practices described in the Vedic texts cannot actually enter into understanding the depths of the Vedic spiritual science, nor acquire the realizations that should accompany it. So, rather than pursuing his research in an academic atmosphere at a university, Stephen directly engaged in the spiritual disciplines that have been recommended for hundreds of years. He continued his study of Vedic knowledge and spiritual practice under the guidance of a spiritual master. Through this process, and with the sanction of His Divine Grace A. C. Bhaktivedanta Swami Prabhupada, he became initiated into the genuine and authorized spiritual line of the Brahma-Madhava-Gaudiya *sampradaya*, which is a disciplic succession that descends back through Sri Caitanya Mahaprabhu and Sri Vyasadeva, the compiler of Vedic literature, and further back to Sri Krishna. Through this initiation he has taken the spiritual name of Sri Nandanandana dasa. Besides being *brahminically* initiated, Stephen has also been to India several times and traveled extensively throughout the country, visiting most of the major holy places and gaining a wide variety of spiritual experiences that only such places can give.

Stephen has written numerous articles, as well as books such as *The Eastern Answers to the Mysteries of Life* series, which includes *The Secret Teachings of the Vedas*, *The Universal Path to Enlightenment*, *The Vedic Prophecies*, and *How the Universe was Created and Our Purpose In It*. He has also written *Toward World Peace: Seeing the Unity Between Us All*, *Facing Death: Welcoming the Afterlife*, *The*

Key to Real Happiness, Proof of Vedic Culture's Global Existence., Reincarnation and Karma: How They Really Affect Us, and *The Heart of Hinduism: The Eastern Path to Freedom, Empowerment and Illumination.* Furthermore, he has authored a novel, *Destined for Infinity,* for those who prefer lighter reading, or learning spiritual knowledge in the context of an exciting, spiritual adventure. Stephen has put the culmination of over thirty years of continuous research and travel experience into his books in an effort to share it with those who are also looking for spiritual understanding. More books are forthcoming, so stay in touch through his website to find out further developments at: http://www.stephen-knapp.com.

If you have enjoyed this book, or if you are serious about finding higher levels of real spiritual Truth, you will also want to get:

The Secret Teachings of the Vedas

This book presents the essence of the ancient Eastern philosophy and summarizes some of the most elevated and important of all spiritual knowledge. This enlightening information is explained in a clear and concise way and is essential for all who want to increase their spiritual understanding, regardless of what their religious background may be. If you are looking for a book to give you an in-depth introduction to the Vedic spiritual knowledge, and to get you started in real spiritual understanding, this is the book!

The topics include: What is your real spiritual identity; the Vedic explanation of the soul; scientific evidence that consciousness is separate from but interacts with the body; the real unity between us all; how to attain the highest happiness and freedom from the cause of suffering; the law of karma and reincarnation; the karma of a nation; where you are really going in life; the real process of progressive evolution; life after death—heaven, hell, or beyond; a description of the spiritual realm; the nature of the Absolute Truth—personal God or impersonal force; recognizing the existence of the Supreme; the reason why we exist at all; and much more. This book provides the answers to questions not found in other religions or philosophies, and condenses information from a wide variety of sources that would take a person years to assemble. It also contains many quotations from the Vedic texts to let the texts speak for themselves, and to show the knowledge the Vedas have held for thousands of years. It also explains the history and origins of the Vedic literature. This book has been called one of the best reviews of Eastern philosophy available.

The Vedic Prophecies:
A New Look into the Future

The Vedic prophecies take you to the end of time! This is the first book ever to present the unique predictions found in the ancient Vedic texts of India. These prophecies are like no others and will provide you with a very different view of the future and how things fit together in the plan for the universe.

Now you can discover the amazing secrets that are hidden in the oldest spiritual writings on the planet. Find out what they say about the distant future, and what the seers of long ago saw in their visions of the destiny of the world.

This book will reveal predictions of deteriorating social changes and how to avoid them; future droughts and famines; low-class rulers and evil governments; whether there will be another appearance (second coming) of God; and predictions of a new spiritual awareness and how it will spread around the world. You will also learn the answers to such questions as:

- Does the future get worse or better?
- Will there be future world wars or global disasters?
- What lies beyond the predictions of Nostradamus, the Mayan prophecies, or the Biblical apocalypse?
- Are we in the end times? How to recognize them if we are.
- Does the world come to an end? If so, when and how?

Now you can find out what the future holds. The Vedic Prophecies carry an important message and warning for all humanity, which needs to be understood now!

Toward World Peace:
Seeing the Unity Between Us All

This book points out the essential reasons why peace in the world and cooperation amongst people, communities, and nations have been so difficult to establish. It also advises the only way real peace and harmony amongst humanity can
be achieved.

In order for peace and unity to exist we must first realize what barriers and
divisions keep us apart. Only then can we break through those barriers to see the
unity that naturally exists between us all. Then, rather than focus on our differences, it is easier to recognize our similarities and common goals. With a common goal established, all of humanity can work together to help each other reach
that destiny.

This book is short and to the point. It is a thought provoking book and will
provide inspiration for anyone. It is especially useful for those working in politics,
religion, interfaith, race relations, the media, the United Nations, teaching, or
who have a position of leadership in any capacity. It is also for those of us who
simply want to spread the insights needed for bringing greater levels of peace,
acceptance, unity, and equality between friends, neighbours, and communities.
Such insights include:

• The factors that keep us apart.
• Breaking down cultural distinctions.
• Breaking down the religious differences.
• Seeing through bodily distinctions.
• We are all working to attain the same things.
• Our real identity: The basis for common ground.
• Seeing the Divinity within each of us.
• What we can do to bring unity between everyone we meet.

This book carries an important message and plan of action that we must
incorporate into our lives and plans for the future if we intend to ever bring peace
and unity between us.

Facing Death
Welcoming the Afterlife

Many people are afraid of death, or do not know how to prepare for it nor what to expect. So this book is provided to relieve anyone of the fear that often accompanies the thought of death, and to supply a means to more clearly understand the purpose of it and how we can use it to our advantage. It will also help the survivors of the departed souls to better understand what has happened and how to cope with it. Furthermore, it shows that death is not a tragedy, but a natural course of events meant to help us reach our destiny.

This book is easy to read, with soothing and comforting wisdom, along with stories of people who have been with departing souls and what they have experienced. It is written especially for those who have given death little thought beforehand, but now would like to have some preparedness for what may need to be done regarding the many levels of the experience and what might take place during this transition.

To assist you in preparing for your own death, or that of a loved one, you will find guidelines for making one's final days as peaceful and as smooth as possible, both physically and spiritually. Preparing for death, no matter what stage of life you are in, can transform your whole outlook in a positive way, if understood properly. This will make things clearer in regard to what matters most in this life, especially when you know the remainder of your life may be short. It is like looking into the Truth of yourself, and taking a pilgrimage to the edge of the spiritual dimension. Some of the topics in the book include:

- The fear of death and learning to let go.
- The opportunity of death: The portal into the next life.
- This earth and this body are no one's real home, so death is natural.
- Being practical and dealing with the final responsibilities.
- Forgiving yourself and others before you go.
- Being the assistant of one leaving this life.
- Connecting with the person inside the disease.
- Surviving the death of a loved one.
- Stories of being with dying, and an amazing near-death-experience.
- Connecting to the spiritual side of death.
- What happens while leaving the body.
- What difference the consciousness makes during death, and how to attain the best level of awareness to carry you through it, or what death will be like and how to prepare for it, this book will help you.

The Key to Real Happiness

This book is actually a guide to one of the prime purposes of life. Naturally everyone wants to be happy. Why else do we keep living and working? Now you can find greater levels of happiness and fulfillment. Using this knowledge from the East, you can get clear advice on the path for reaching an independent and uninterrupted feeling of well-being. This information is sure to open your eyes to higher possibilities. It can awaken you to the natural joy that always exists within your higher Self.

Many people consider happiness as something found with the increase of sensual pleasure and comforts. Others look for position, or ease of living, thrills, or more money and what it can buy. However, by using knowledge from the East and taking an alternative look at what is advised herein, we get guidance on our true position and the means necessary for reaching the happiness for which we always hanker. Some of the topics include:

- What keeps us from being truly happy.
- Your spiritual Self is beyond all temporary material limitations.
- How to uplift your consciousness.
- How all suffering exists only within the illusion, and what is illusion.
- How your thoughts and consciousness create your future and determine your state of happiness and outlook on life.
- Wrong ambitions and their hidden results.
- How to defend yourself from negativity.
- How real independent and self-sufficient happiness is already within you, and how to unveil it.
- How to enjoy that ever-existing pleasure within.

This book is easy to understand and will show you how to experience real happiness and reach the spiritual level, the platform of the soul, beyond the temporary nature of the mind and body.

Proof of Vedic Culture's Global Existence

This book provides evidence which makes it clear that the ancient Vedic culture was once a global society. Even today we can see its influence in any part of the world. Thus, it becomes obvious that before the world became full of distinct and separate cultures, religions and countries, it was once united in a common brotherhood of Vedic culture, with common standards, principles, and representations of God.

No matter what we may consider our present religion, society or country, we are all descendants of this ancient global civilization. Thus, the Vedic culture is the parent of all humanity and the original ancestor of all religions. In this way, we all share a common heritage.

This book is an attempt to allow humanity to see more clearly its universal roots. This book provides a look into:

- How Vedic knowledge was given to humanity by the Supreme.
- The history and traditional source of the Vedas and Vedic Aryan society.
- Who were the original Vedic Aryans. How Vedic society was a global influence and what shattered this world-wide society. How Sanskrit faded from being a global language.
- Many scientific discoveries over the past several centuries are only rediscoveries of what the Vedic literature already knew.
- How the origins of world literature are found in India and Sanskrit.
- The links between the Vedic and other ancient cultures, such as the Sumerians, Persians, Egyptians, Romans, Greeks, and others.
- Links between the Vedic tradition and Judaism, Christianity, Islam, and Buddhism.
- How many of the western holy sites, churches, and mosques were once the sites of Vedic holy places and sacred shrines.
- The Vedic influence presently found in such countries as Britain, France, Russia, Greece, Israel, Arabia, China, Japan, and in areas of Scandinavia, the Middle East, Africa, the South Pacific, and the Americas.
- Uncovering the truth of India's history: Powerful evidence that shows how many mosques and Muslim buildings were once opulent Vedic temples, including the Taj Mahal, Delhi's Jama Masjid, Kutab Minar, as well as buildings in many other cities, such as Agra, Ahmedabad, Bijapur, etc.
- How there is presently a need to plan for the survival of Vedic culture.

This book is sure to provide some amazing facts and evidence about the truth of world history and the ancient, global Vedic Culture. This book has enough startling information and historical evidence to cause a major shift in the way we view religious history and the basis of world traditions.

Destined for Infinity

Deep within the mystical and spiritual practices of India are doors that lead to various levels of both higher and lower planes of existence. Few people from the outside are ever able to enter into the depths of these practices to experience such levels of reality.

This is the story of the mystical adventure of a man, Roman West, who entered deep into the secrets of India where few other Westerners have been able to penetrate. While living with a master in the Himalayan foothills and traveling the mystical path that leads to the Infinite, he witnesses the amazing powers the mystics can achieve and undergoes some of the most unusual experiences of his life. Under the guidance of a master that he meets in the mountains, he gradually develops mystic abilities of his own and attains the sacred vision of the enlightened sages and enters the unfathomable realm of Infinity. However, his peaceful life in the hills comes to an abrupt end when he is unexpectedly forced to confront the powerful forces of darkness that have been unleashed by an evil Tantric priest to kill both Roman and his master. His only chance to defeat the intense forces of darkness depends on whatever spiritual strength he has been able to develop.

This story includes traditions and legends that have existed for hundreds and thousands of years. All of the philosophy, rituals, mystic powers, forms of meditation, and descriptions of the Absolute are authentic and taken from narrations found in many of the sacred books of the East, or gathered by the author from his own experiences in India and information from various sages themselves.

This book will will prepare you to perceive the multi-dimensional realities that exist all around us, outside our sense perception. This is a book that will give you many insights into the broad possibilities of our life and purpose in this world.

Published by iUniverse.com, $16.95, 255 Pages, ISBN: 0-595-33959-X.

Reincarnation and Karma: How They Really Affect Us

Everyone may know a little about reincarnation, but few understand the complexities and how it actually works. Now you can find out how reincarnation and karma really affect us. Herein all of the details are provided on how a person is implicated for better or worse by their own actions. You will understand why particular situations in life happen, and how to make improvements for one's future. You will see why it appears that bad things happen to good people, or even why good things happen to bad people, and what can be done about it.

Other topics include:

- Reincarnation recognized throughout the world
- The most ancient teachings on reincarnation
- Reincarnation in Christianity
- How we transmigrate from one body to another
- Life between lives
- Going to heaven or hell
- The reason for reincarnation
- Free will and choice
- Karma of the nation
- How we determine our own destiny
- What our next life may be like
- Becoming free from all karma and how to prepare to make our next life the best possible.

Combine this with modern research into past life memories and experiences and you will have a complete view of how reincarnation and karma really operate. Published by iUniverse.com, $13.95, 135 pages, ISBN: 0-595-34199-3.

The Heart of Hinduism

This is a definitive and easy to understand guide to the essential as well as devotional heart of the Vedic/Hindu philosophy. You will see the depths of wisdom and insights that are contained within this profound spiritual knowledge. This presentation contains numerous references from a variety of the ancient Vedic texts to provide a direct view of the spiritual knowledge that they hold. Thus, it is especially good for anyone who lacks the time to research the many topics that are contained within the numerous Vedic manuscripts and to see the advantages of knowing them. This also provides you with a complete process for progressing on the spiritual path, making way for individual empowerment, freedom, and spiritual illumination. All the information is now at your fingertips.

Some of the topics you will find include:

- A complete review of all the Vedic texts and the wide range of topics they contain. This also presents the traditional origins of the Vedic philosophy and how it was developed, and their philosophical conclusion.
- The uniqueness and freedom of the Vedic system.
- A description of the main yoga processes and their effectiveness.
- A review of the Vedic Gods, such as Krishna, Shiva, Durga, Ganesh, and others. You will learn the identity and purpose of each.
- You will have the essential teachings of Lord Krishna who has given some of the most direct and insightful of all spiritual messages known to humanity, and the key to direct spiritual perception.
- The real purpose of yoga and the religious systems.
- What is the most effective spiritual path for this modern age and what it can do for you, with practical instructions for deep realizations.
- The universal path of devotion, the one world religion.
- How Vedic culture is the last bastion of deep spiritual truth.
- Plus many more topics and information for your enlightenment.

So to dive deep into what is Hinduism and the Vedic path to freedom and spiritual perception, this book will give you a jump start. Knowledge is the process of personal empowerment, and no knowledge will give you more power than deep spiritual understanding. And those realizations described in the Vedic culture are the oldest and some of the most profound that humanity has ever known.

Published by iUniverse.com, $35.95, 650 pages, ISBN: 0-595-35075-5.

Vedic Culture
The Difference It Can Make In Your Life

The Vedic culture of India is rooted in Sanatana-dharma, the eternal and universal truths that are beneficial to everyone. It includes many avenues of self-development that an increasing number of people from the West are starting to investigate and use, including:

- Yoga
- Meditation and spiritual practice
- Vedic astrology
- Ayurveda
- Vedic gemology
- Vastu or home arrangement
- Environmental awareness
- Vegetarianism
- Social cooperation and arrangement
- The means for global peace
- And much more

Vedic Culture: The Difference It Can Make In Your Life shows the advantages of the Vedic paths of improvement and self-discovery that you can use in your life to attain higher personal awareness, happiness, and fulfillment. It also provides a new view of what these avenues have to offer from some of the most prominent writers on Vedic culture in the West, who discovered how it has affected and benefited their own lives. They write about what it has done for them and then explain how their particular area of interest can assist others. The noted authors include, David Frawley, Subhash Kak, Chakrapani Ullal, Michael Cremo, Jeffrey Armstrong, Robert Talyor, Howard Beckman, Andy Fraenkel, George Vutetakis, Pratichi Mathur, Dhan Rousse, Arun Naik, Parama Karuna Devi, and Stephen Knapp, all of whom have numerous authored books or articles of their own.

For the benefit of individuals and social progress, the Vedic system is as relevant today as it was in ancient times. Discover why there is a growing renaissance in what the Vedic tradition has to offer in *Vedic Culture*.

Published by iUniverse.com, $22.95, 312 pages, ISBN: 0-595-37120-5.

www.Stephen-Knapp.com

Be sure to visit Stephen's web site. It provides lots of information on many spiritual aspects of Vedic and spiritual philosophy, and Indian culture for both beginners and the scholarly.

You will find all the descriptions and contents of Stephen's books, how to order them, and keep up with any new books or articles that he has written.

There is also a page with reviews and unsolicited letters from readers who have expressed their appreciation for his books, as well as his website. Find out what they have said. Free online booklets are also available for your use or distribution on meditation, why be a Hindu, who is Krishna, who is Shiva and Durga, a review of the Vedic texts, death of the Aryan invasion theory, and others. There is also a free online book of helpful prayers, mantras, gayatris and devotional songs for your use.

There are numerous enlightening articles and excerpts from his books that can help answer many questions about life, the process of spiritual development, the basics of the Vedic path, or how to broaden our spiritual awareness. Many of these are emailed among friends or posted on other web sites. Articles include: Spiritual Enlightenment: A Cure for Social Ills, The Purpose of Life, Seeing the Divinity Within Everyone, World Peace is a Possibility, Dispelling the Fear of Death, Your Thoughts Create Your Future, Seeing Beyond the Illusion, Similarities Between Christianity and Hinduism, When Religions Create Divisions and How to Avoid Them, and many more about the truth of spiritual reality and Vedic culture.

There is also "Seeing Spiritual India," an introduction to traveling to the holy places of India with over 100 color photos taken by Stephen. There are also descriptions and 40 photos of the huge and amazing Kumbha Mela festival.

There are also directories of many Krishna and Hindu temples around the world to help you locate one near you, where you can continue your experience along the Eastern path. There are postings of the recent archeological discoveries that confirm the Vedic version of history. There is a photographic exhibit of the Vedic influence in the Taj Mahal, questioning whether it was built by Shah Jahan. There is also a large list of links to additional websites to help you continue your exploration of Eastern philosophy, or provide more information and news about India, Hinduism, ancient Vedic culture, Vaishnavism, Hare Krishna sites, travel, visas, catalogs for books and paraphernalia, holy places, etc.

There is also a large resource for vegetarian recipes, information on its benefits, how to get started, ethnic stores, or non-meat ingredients and supplies.

You will also find a large "Krishna Darshan Art Gallery" of photos and prints of Krishna and Vedic divinities. You can also find a large collection of previously unpublished photos of His Divine Grace A. C. Bhaktivedanta Swami.

This site is made as a practical resource for your use and is continually being updated and expanded with more articles, resources, and information. Be sure to check it out.

978-0-595-39352
0-595-39352-7

Printed in the United Kingdom
by Lightning Source UK Ltd.
114704UKS00001B/114